PAINTING Heartwarming
Holidays

4 Seasons of Painting with Jamie Mills-Price

NORTH LIGHT BOOKS
CINCINNATI, OHIO
WWW.ARTISTSNETWORK.COM

Other fine North Light Books are available from your local bookstore, art sup-
ply store or direct from the publisher.

10 09 08 07 06   5 4 3

Distributed in Canada by Fraser Direct
100 Armstrong Avenue
Georgetown, ON, Canada L7G 5S4
Tel: (905) 877-4411

Distributed in the U.K. and Europe by David & Charles
Brunel House, Newton Abbot, Devon, TQ12 4PU, England
Tel: (+44) 1626 323200, Fax: (+44) 1626 323319
Email: mail@davidandcharles.co.uk

Distributed in Australia by Capricorn Link
P.O. Box 704, S. Windsor NSW, 2756 Australia
Tel: (02) 4577-3555

Library of Congress Cataloging-in-Publication Data

Mills-Price, Jamie.
  Painting heartwarming holidays : 4 seasons of painting with Jamie Mills-Price
/ Jamie Mills Price.-- 1st ed.
      p. cm.
  Includes index.
  ISBN-13 978-1-58180-788-2 (pbk. : alk. paper)
  ISBN-10 1-58180-788-0 (pbk. : alk. paper)
  1. Painting--Technique. 2. Decoration and ornament. I. Title.
  TT385.M58 2006
  745.7'23--dc22
                          2005022303

Editor: Holly Davis
Production Coordinator: Kristen Heller
Designer: Clare Finney
Interior Layout Artist: Kathy Bergstrom
Photographer: Christine Polomsky

ABOUT THE AUTHOR

Jamie Mills-Price is an
increasingly popular dec-
orative painter, designer,
teacher and publisher.
She is the president of
her company, Between
the Vines™, Inc., has cre-
ated numerous painting
packets, is an ongoing
contributor to painting
and craft magazines and
has authored twelve
painting books. She teaches regularly at conventions
and has been invited to teach her seminars across the
United States as well as in Canada, Europe, Mexico, South
America and Japan.

Jamie discovered the joy of painting in 1989, when,
after losing her husband, a friend talked her into taking a
"tole" painting class to help take her mind off her sorrows.
It worked! Jamie soon began painting anything that
stood still. Her active imagination and sense of humor
come across in her whimsical designs and characters.
Designing is Jamie's true passion. She now spends most
of her time creating unique and distinctive whimsical
designs for her books and the gift industry. She has two
sons and lives in beautiful southern Oregon.

For contact information, see Resources, page 126.

METRIC CONVERSION CHART

to convert	to	multiply by
Inches	Centimeters	2.54
Centimeters	Inches	0.40
Feet	Centimeters	30.50
Centimeters	Feet	0.03
Yards	Meters	0.90
Meters	Yards	1.10

DEDICATION

I would like to dedicate this book to my parents.

Mom and Dad, thank you for being so wonderful and loving. Through all the creative endeavors in my life, you have stood by me and given me your support.

Thank you for giving me the wings to fly. I love and appreciate you both.

ACKNOWLEDGMENTS

I would like to thank all of my family for their love and support and my good friends for their help in getting this book together.

Special thanks go to my two sons, Ryan and Tyler; I love you both and am very proud of the fine young men you've turned out to be.

Don, thank you for all your love and support. Flo, I thank you for being there, always ready to assist and guide. Phyllis, I thank you so much for all of your help!

Thank you to DecoArt and Loew-Cornell for their generosity in supplying me with paint and brushes.

A big thank you to the staff at North Light—Kathy Kipp, Holly Davis and Christine Polomsky. You've made the experience of writing this book an enjoyable one!

contents

SUMMER

AUTUMN

WINTER

introduction

Painting Heartwarming Holidays covers all four seasons as well as most major holidays—a whole year of painting enjoyment and creative exploration. Unlocking the creativity we all hold inside not only leads to exciting discoveries but is also beneficial mentally and emotionally. Losing yourself in a painting project lets you escape reality and enter the world of whimsy and fantasy. Worries and cares seem to float away.

For those of you who are new to or less experienced with decorative painting, the basic instructional material in the beginning of the book (pages 8-21) will get you off to a good start. Don't be afraid—jump in and join the fun! If you're intimidated by a project, try singling out an element from the design for a simpler challenge.

If you're feeling adventurous, you may want to combine elements from different designs to create an all new design. "Designing," on pages 18 to 21, shows a portion of my creative thought process when pulling a design together. This section gives you ideas on how to combine elements to come up with a whole new design. I don't follow rules when I design; I just let my imagination flow freely and have fun. If the resulting design makes me smile, then I know I've succeeded.

Even if you paint my designs just as they are, you can still give them your own creative stamp. I encourage you to experiment with color schemes to suit your own home décor. Note also that I had no special surfaces in mind when creating the designs. Visit your local craft or hobby store or check out the suppliers listed under "Resources" (page 126) for ideas. For unique surfaces, try your local thrift stores, flea markets or auction houses. Pages 10 and 11 give you general information on preparing and finishng different surfaces.

Design, color and surface possibilities are endless! Let yourself go. Nothing compares to the satisfaction of creating a one-of-a-kind treasure to keep for yourself or to give to a friend or loved one. My fervent hope is that the designs and painting instruction in this book will spark the creativity you have inside and that you'll lose yourself in many hours of painting pleasure.

Happy Painting!

Jamie Mills-Price

7

materials

The next few pages are an overview of materials needed to complete the projects in this book. At the beginning of each project, you'll find specific material lists outlining the needs for a particular design.

PATTERN TRANSFER MATERIALS

- **Tracing paper** - This paper is used for tracing the pattern so it can be transferred onto your painting surface.
- **Graphite paper** - This paper works like carbon paper, except it's erasable. Place it on the painting surface with the graphite facing down, using light graphite paper for dark surfaces and dark graphite paper for light surfaces. Then put the pattern on top, taping it in place, if necessary, to keep it from shifting.
- **Stylus, pen or pencil** - Transfer only the pattern lines you need with a stylus, pen or pencil. I recommend a stylus, which can also be used for making paint dots. Whatever tool you use, avoid pressing too hard on wood, or you will etch the design onto the surface.

PAINTING MATERIALS

- **DecoArt Americana Acrylic Paint** - I prefer these paints because the colors are creamy and they cover nicely. See the project material lists for specific colors used.
- **Loew-Cornell brushes** - Your project will turn out only as good as your brushes. See the sidebar on page 9 for more information.
- **Wet palette** - A Sta-Wet Palette by Masterson is wonderful for keeping your acrylics from drying too quickly.
- **Palette paper** - I use a waxed, disposable paper palette for blending my floats. This paper comes in a tablet with tear-off sheets.
- **Loew-Cornell brush basin** - This wonderful water container for rinsing brushes has a grid along the bottom to help remove the paint. Rub the ferrule (metal part of the brush) along the grid and the vibration will shake out the paint.

MORE ABOUT BRUSHES

Loew-Cornell produces excellent art brushes that wear well. I've used them from day one. On the opposite page you see the types of brushes used for this book. For specific project needs, see that project's brush list.

Good brushes require good care. DecoMagic by DecoArt is an all-purpose cleaner that removes paint from brushes, hands, stencils and more. If you run out of cleaner and need something in a pinch, an instant hand-sanitizer (like Purell) will also do the job.

BASICS

In addition to paint and brushes, you should have these materials on hand for every project. Read more about them on these two pages.

• Tracing paper	• Brush basin
• Graphite paper	• Paper towels
• Stylus	• Disposable wipes
• Pen or pencil	• Hair dryer
• Palette	• Eraser

ADDITIONAL MATERIALS

- **Sanding pad or paper** - Use one of these to sand wood surfaces in preparation for painting (see page 10).
- **DecoArt Multi-Purpose Sealer** - Wood, metal and glass should be sealed before they're painted (see pages 10-11).
- **Foam brush** - Apply sealer with a 1-inch (25mm) or 1½-inch (38mm) foam brush.
- **Paper towels** - These come in handy for cleaning up spilled paint, absorbing excess water from brushes and much more. Your paper towels should be soft, absorbent and lint-free. I like the Viva brand. Blue shop towels also work well.
- **Disposable wipes** - These are wonderful for removing acrylic paint from your work area or your hands.
- **Hair dryer** - A handheld dryer speeds up the drying time of your paint and finishes.

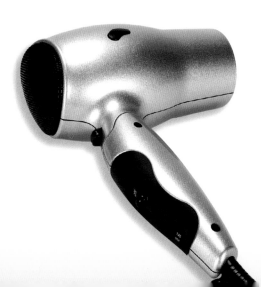

- **Toothbrush** - An ordinary toothbrush works great for creating a spattering of fine dots (see photo demonstration on page 16).
- **Brass stencils** - Two projects in this book, "Americana" and "Holiday Tree," use brass stencils. Specific information about these stencils is in the project material lists.
- **DecoArt Snow-Tex** - This paint medium creates a dimensional snow effect.
- **Eraser** - After painting and before varnishing, use a good art eraser to remove excess graphite lines
- **DecoArt DuraClear Varnish** - I love finishing projects on wood and metal with brush-on varnish as opposed to spray varnish. Use either the satin or matte finish, whichever you prefer, and follow the manufacturer's instructions.
- **Large, soft varnishing brush** - Set aside a ¾-inch (19mm) flat/wash to be used only for varnishing. Don't use a foam brush.

liner, series 7350C

script liner, series 7050

spotter, series 7650

round, series 7000

round stroke, series 7040

Debbie Mitchell stippler, series DM

Filbert, series 7500C

crescent, series 247

Maxine's oval mop, series 270

flat/shader, series 7300C

flat/wash, series 7550

9

surface preparation and finishing

Projects in this book can be painted on many different surfaces. Feel free to enlarge or reduce the design patterns to fit different surface sizes—just keep in mind that you may need to adjust your brush size. You can also select just a portion of a design for your project. Experiment and have fun!

Different surfaces require different preparation and finishing. The following brief explanations for five common surfaces—wood, fabric, metal, glass and paper—may be all the information you need. If you have further questions, consult someone at your local paint, hobby or craft store.

WOOD

Check for dents or holes in your wood surface and fill them with wood filler. Once the filler is dry, sand the surface smooth, moving with the woodgrain. Wipe off the sanding dust with a paper towel.

When the surface is smooth and dust free, use a 1-inch (25mm) or 1½-inch (38mm) foam brush to apply sealer, such as DecoArt Multi-Purpose Sealer The sealer will raise the grain a bit, so after it dries, sand the surface again lightly (moving with the grain of the wood). Wipe off the sanding dust with a paper towel.

At this point you're ready to apply a basecoat, as specified by your project directions. Paint the entire project and let it dry.

To finish a wood surface, apply a good varnish like DecoArt's DuraClear, either in satin or matte finish. Apply varnish with a large, soft brush (not foam) according to the manufacturer's directions.

FABRIC

Generally, before painting on fabric you should wash it to remove the sizing. Do not add softener to your wash! Mix fabric painting medium with your regular acrylics, following the manufacturer's instructions. You may prefer using specialized fabric paint, which will make the design more pliable than fabric painting medium. Both fabric paint and fabric paint medium promote better adherence of the paint to the fabric, help prevent cracking and enable ordinary laundering.

When you've finished painting the project, set the design by ironing the fabric.

Use One or the Other
When painting on fabric, either add fabric painting medium to your regular acrylic paints or use specialized fabric paint.

METAL

Prepare the metal surface by wiping it down with a solution of vinegar and water (1:1). Let the surface dry, and then brush on one coat of DecoArt Multi-Purpose Sealer, which will act as a primer. A spray primer from your local hardware store can also be used.

Apply your acrylic paints in an even manner. Metal is not porous, so the brush strokes will show if you apply the paint too thickly. I prefer layering several thin coats to get a smooth surface.

When you've completed your project, finish your metal piece with varnish as you would for a wood surface.

PAPER

No preparation is necessary for painting on paper. Just keep in mind that paper is porous, and you may need to work with a bit more water in your brush than usual. No finishing is necessary, either, although you may use a spray fixative.

GLASS

Special glass paints are available in colors similar to the normal acrylic palette. Follow the preparation and finishing instructions given by the paint manufacturer.

techniques

The next few pages are an overview of the brush loads, floats, strokes and other techniques used throughout this book. A little practice up front can make a big difference in your finished painting. You can also refer to this section to refresh your memory as you're working on a project .

Full Load

Use this brush load when none is specified. Basecoating is a common use.

1. LOAD
Load one side of the brush. Then turn the brush and load the other side.

2. WORK INTO BRISTLES
Wipe the brush on a palette to work the paint into the bristles.

Side Load

I use this load for most floating techniques—shading, highlighting and tinting.

1. LOAD
Load one corner of the brush.

2. WORK INTO BRISTLES
Work the paint into the bristles by stroking on the palette.

Double Load

I use this load for leaves, roses and stippling.

1. LOAD FIRST COLOR
Load one side of the brush in the first color.

2. LOAD SECOND COLOR
Turn the brush over and load the second color on the other side of the brush.

3. BLEND
 Blend the colors on the palette.

Triple Load

I use this load for leaves, flowers and various stippling techniques.

1. LOAD FIRST COLOR
Fully load the first color and work it into the bristles on the palette.

2. LOAD SECOND COLOR
Load the second color on one brush corner.

3. LOAD THIRD COLOR
Load the third color on the opposite brush corner.

4. BLEND
Blend the three colors on the palette.

A WORD ABOUT FLOATS

Floating is the term I use when I shade, highlight or tint areas of a design to give dimension and interest. I generally float with a water-dampened brush and only a small amount of side-loaded paint. Blend the paint on your palette until you achieve a soft graduation of color.

Dabby Float

1. TAP TAP TAP
Tap the brush repeatedly.

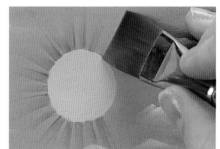

2. USE THIS FLOAT . . .
Use this float when you want to give an area texture, such as on a Teddy Bear's fur or in grassy areas.

Stutter Float

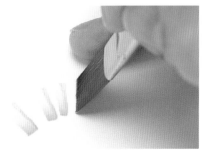

1. TOUCH AND LIFT
Touch down, lift and touch down repeatedly.

2. USE THIS FLOAT . . .
Use this float to create a separated float effect, as with rays around a sun or star shine.

Side-by-Side Float

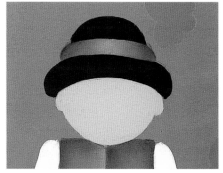

1. FLOAT ONCE
Float the color (see "A Word About Floats" on the previous page).

2. FLOAT AGAIN
Float again right beside the first float.

3. USE THIS FLOAT . . .
Use this technique to create a soft seamless float in areas that have no hard edge, such as the highlight on the hatband.

Bull's-Eye Float

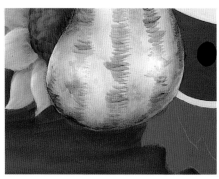

1. PIVOT AND TAP
Tap to create a circular effect, keeping the color edge of the brush pivoting on the inside and the water edge of the brush on the outside. Lifting the brush as you float creates a casual effect.

2. USE THIS FLOAT . . .
Use this float to create casual "circles" of color, like the highlights and tints on this gourd.

Line Pulling and Vining

1. USE YOUR PINKY
When pulling a line, rest your pinky on the painting surface to steady your hand.

2. PRESS AND RELEASE FOR VINES
For the thick-and-thin effect used to paint vines, roll the brush on your middle finger as you pull. As you do this, alternate pressing down and releasing the pressure. When you press, the line line gets thicker; when you release, it gets thinner.

Tap Stipple

1. LOAD
Unless otherwise directed, double load a stippler (see page 12).

2. BLEND
Tap the brush on the palette to blend the two colors.

3. TAP
Tap the brush on the painting to stipple in the color.

4. USE THIS STIPPLE . . .
Use this stipple anywhere you need lots of texture, such as with bushes or flowery trees.

Drybrush Scrub

1. LOAD
Load a small amount of paint on one corner of a dry stippler.

2. SWIRL
Swirl the bristles on the palette to distribute the paint evenly.

3. SCRUB
Scrub on a paper towel in a swirling manner.

4. SCRUB AGAIN
Scrub on the color. Use this technique to create soft touches of color, such as cheeks.

Stylus and Liner Dots

1. DOT WITH STYLUS
To create evenly shaped dots, use a paint-tipped stylus.

2. DOT WITH BRUSH
To create softer, less uniform dots, use a paint-tipped brush.

Toothbrush Spatter

1. DIP
Dip the toothbrush in water and then in a puddle of paint.

2. SWIRL
Use the toothbrush to swirl the water and paint together on the palette.

3. SPATTER
Run your finger along the toothbrush bristles to spatter the paint.

4. USE SPATTERING . . .
Use toothbrush spattering to create a soft spray of dots, such as for falling snow or for background speckling. A tissue covering keeps spatters off other parts of the painting

C-Stroke

1. TOUCH, PRESS AND PULL
Start on the chisel (ends of the brush bristles) and pull, pressing lightly and curving.

2. LIFT OFF
To end the stroke, lift onto the brush chisel.

Shrimp Stroke

1. TOUCH DOWN AND PULL
Start on the chisel and pull a line.

2. LIFT AND REPEAT
Lift the brush and then again come down on the chisel and pull.

3. CONTINUE
Repeat as often as necessary

4. USE THIS STROKE . . .
You can use the shrimp stroke combined with two C-strokes to create a rose. The C-strokes form the rose's "bowl"; the shrimp strokes form the rose's "skirt" (see page 38).

Stroke Leaf

1. TOUCH, PRESS AND PULL
Touch down on the chisel, press and pull. Strive for a diamond shape.

2. LIFT OFF
Finish the leaf by lifting off onto the chisel.

3. USE THIS STROKE . . .
The stroke leaf is one method of creating leaves on flowers and vines, such as the green leaves on these berry branches.

designing

Part of the fun of decorative painting is adding your personal creative touch. One way you can do this is to alter existing designs or develop your own. How do you go about this? I don't have a formula for designing, but I can share with you a few insights and a couple of examples of how my designs come together.

One Idea Leads to Another

There's no rhyme or reason to my design creativity. I simply start visualizing, put my pencil to paper and let my mind flow. Sometimes one idea leads to another until I end up with a design I never would have imagined at the beginning of my creative journey. "Pumpkin Pull Toy" began as I was trying to think of a fun new autumn design. I started by sketching a basic pumpkin.

While looking at the pumpkin sitting all by itself, I brainstormed about what to do with it. Did I want to make it whimsical with a birdhouse opening and twisting vines? Did I want to use it in an autumn scene? Should I combine the pumpkin with other fall elements? I decided I'd try a pumpkin cottage, complete with a window, window boxes and shutters.

Then I got to thinking how funny the pumpkin would look sitting on a big ear of corn. (Who but me would think of such a thing?!) Could I make this whimsy work without it being (pardon the pun) too corny? At worst I'd just erase it. Nothing is against the rules.

So I added the corn and thought, Hmmm, what about making it a pull toy? A set of wheels and a pull string was all it needed. I was on a roll!

I adore detail, so I started thinking of what else I could add to round out the design. How about a few sunflowers peeking from behind? What about a vine wrapping around the pumpkin? Either would work for me. Which to choose? I considered the color scheme I had going and decided sunflowers would look better next to the pumpkin.

This was turning out pretty fun! But I asked myself if the design was balanced. Should I add something else? What and where? That's when the idea of a flag popped into my head. I sketched the flag and added vines around the flag pole (vines always seem to make their way into my designs). To this I added grass and a few vines and greenery in the window box. Finally the design looked just right.

All I had left to do was the painting.

PUMPKIN PULL TOY

Here a Sketch, There a Sketch

Doodling is a favorite pastime of mine, so I have an abundance of sketches at my fingertips. I used to sketch on anything available—receipts, envelopes, napkins—whatever was handy. I couldn't keep track of all those bits of paper lying around, so through the years I've learned to grab for my sketchbook when I feel the urge to draw. That way I know right where to look for designing ideas.

"Honey Bear" is a compilation of sketches drawn at different times. One of those was this beehive—a simple little shape with a softly flowing vine around it.

Here's another original sketch of a birdhouse, rather plain except for the vine twisting around the post.

I love the way vines can be used to fill in and round out a design, such as this one.

I added a flower atop the birdhouse, in keeping with the floral-enhanced theme started with the bee-hive. Polka dots on the roof and simple stripes through the house set it off nicely.

I altered that original sketch by adding a flower on top and changing to a more angular vine.

This dear little bear was originally sketched with a flower in his hand, another in his belly button and a bow around his neck.

I combined the bear with the bird-house and beehive, adding a few bees and flowers and adjusting the vine. I thought the bear's bow would be too much with the vine, so I removed it, along with the bear's flowers. I added simple stitching lines on his body, arms, legs and feet.

Here's the painting of the completed design, the compilation of a sketch here and a sketch there.

HONEY BEAR

Spring Wreath

OH LOVELY SPRING! What a beautiful time of year, with flowers in bloom, new greenery appearing on the trees and baby birds peeking their heads out of the nest.

This is the first of four seasonal wreaths, each showing the same scene at a different time of year. In the spring wreath, the flowerlike palette colors bring out the beauty of springtime, the nest reflects the tans and browns of nature and the soft, blue eggs signal life forthcoming. For a bolder celebration of color, paint the tulips a bit brighter. If you would like a sun peeking over the valley, simply paint the sky from the summer wreath. Add or eliminate elements from the four seasonal wreaths to suit your taste.

PAINT: DECOART AMERICANA ACRYLICS

| Antique Mauve | Antique White | Burnt Umber | Fawn |

| Golden Straw | Hauser Light Green | Jade Green | Lamp Black |

| Light Avocado | Light Buttermilk | Light French Blue | Mississippi Mud |

| Pansy Lavender | Plantation Pine | Raw Sienna | Rookwood Red |

| Uniform Blue | Yellow Ochre |

Materials

LOEW-CORNELL BRUSHES

Flat/wash, series 7550
- ½-inch (13mm)
- ¾-inch (19mm)
- 1-inch (25mm)

Flat/shader, series 7300C
- No. 4
- No. 8
- No. 10

Filbert, series 7500C
- No. 6
- No. 10

Liner, series 7350C
- 18/0
- 10/0

Script liner, series 7050
- 18/0
- No. 1

Round Stroke, series 7040
- No. 2
- No. 4

Debbie Mitchell (DM) stippler, series DM
- ⅛-inch (3mm)
- ¼-inch (6mm)
- ⅜-inch (10mm)

ADDITIONAL MATERIALS

- Basics (See list on page 8.)
- Painting surface of your choice, about 12" x 15" (31cm x 38cm)
- Preparation and finishing materials appropriate for your painting surface (See pages 10-11.)
- Spattering materials: toothbrush and paper to cover painting.

Pattern on page 122.

[1] PREPARE, TRACE AND BASE

Prepare your painting surface (see pages 10-11). Paint the background in a slip-slap manner with a 1-inch (25mm) flat/wash double-loaded with Antique White and Light Buttermilk. Trace the wreath inset and the heart outline onto the surface. Base the hills with a no. 10 filbert and Hauser Light Green + Light Buttermilk. Base the sky with a no. 10 filbert and a double load of Light French Blue and Light Buttermilk. Base the path with a no. 6 filbert and Fawn.

[2] FLOAT IN CLOUDS

Side load a ¾-inch (19mm) flat/wash with Light French Blue + Light Buttermilk and float in the clouds. Do this in several layers, letting the paint dry between each and adding more Light Buttermilk to the mix to brighten highlights. Add a floated horizon line with the same mix.

[3] SHADE AND HIGHLIGHT HILLS

Using the same brush, shade the hills with dabby floats (see page 13) of side-loaded Plantation Pine. These dabby floats create texture.

Still using the same brush and a dabby float, highlight the hills with a side-loaded brush mix of Hauser Light Green + Golden Straw. For lightest highlights, add Light Buttermilk onto the dirty brush.

[4] SHADE SKY

With the same brush, float side-loaded Uniform Blue shading along the upper perimeter of the sky.

[5] SHADE, HIGHLIGHT AND TINT PATH

Move down to a ½-inch (13mm) flat/wash and shade the path with dabby floats of side-loaded Burnt Umber. Using the same brush, add dabby Yellow Ochre highlights along the middle area of the path. Then tint the path edges here and there with side-loaded Plantation Pine. Walk the tints into the path just a bit.

[6] PAINT FIR TRUNKS

Transfer the pattern of the trees, birdhouses, nest, eggs, tulips and other vine flowers. Use dark graphite paper for elements on the light background and light graphite paper for elements in the middle of the wreath. Using an 18/0 liner and Burnt Umber, paint the fir trunks. Load the same brush in Plantation Pine and stroke in the branches. Then tip the dirty brush in Jade Green and paint the branches again.

[7] PAINT TRUNKS AND BRANCHES OF FLOWERING TREES

Paint the trunks and branches of the flowering trees with a no. 2 round stroke brush and Burnt Umber, Lamp Black and Fawn, varying the colors in brush mixes of two or three colors.

[8] STIPPLE FLOWERS AND FLOAT SHADING

Tap stipple (see page 15) the flowers on the two trees on the right with a ¼-inch (6mm) DM stippler. For the right front tree, use a double load of Hauser Light Green and Light Buttermilk. For the right back tree, use a double load of Antique Mauve and Light Buttermilk. Then side load a ½-inch (13mm) flat/wash with Antique Mauve and float in shading where the pink flowers tuck behind the white flowers.

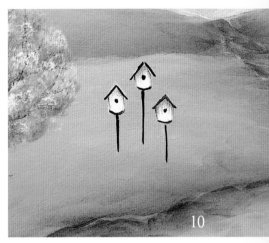

[9] STIPPLE AND SHADE LEFT TREE FLOWERS

Paint the flowering tree on the left with the same tap stippling technique used with the two on the right, but with different colors, brushes and loads. First triple load (see page 13) a ⅜-inch (10mm) DM stippler using Antique Mauve for the full load and Rookwood Red and Light Buttermilk for the side loads. Stipple the flowery foliage and then shade the bottom of this foliage with a ½-inch (13mm) flat/wash side-loaded with Antique Mauve.

[10] PAINT BIRDHOUSES

Base the birdhouses with a 10/0 liner and Light Buttermilk. Shade with a no. 8 flat/shader and Lamp Black. The birdhouse openings are dotted in with the same color on a 10/0 liner. Use the same brush and color to paint the posts, rooftops and bases.

[11] STIPPLE AND ANCHOR

Tap stipple the bushes and shrubs with a ⅛-inch (3mm) DM stippler double-loaded in Plantation Pine and Light Buttermilk. Side load a no. 10 flat/shader with Plantation Pine and float beneath the bushes, shrubs and birdhouses to anchor them to the hills and the path.

[12] ADD ACCENTS, FLOWERS AND GRASSES

Load a 10/0 liner in Plantation Pine, tip in Hauser Light Green and dab on some accent to the bushes and some stippled flowers along the path. Load the same brush with Light Buttermilk and dab on some "candy tuft" bushes. These are the bright white bushes along the path. With the same brush, dab in small flowers along the path and under the trees, loading colors of your choice from the palette and then tipping the brush in Light Buttermilk. Using the 10/0 liner, add some grasses in Jade Green and some in Plantation Pine along the path, under the birdhouses and around the trees.

13

14

15

16

[13] UNDERCOAT NEST AND TULIPS

Undercoat the tulips, nest, eggs and leaves with a no. 6 filbert and Antique White. Tip the brush in Light Buttermilk as needed to create contrast. The yellow tulip at the bottom is already undercoated with the background color.

[14] BASE TULIPS

Basecoat all the tulips and tulip leaves with a no. 6 filbert. These basecoats are washes rather than opaque color. Use Yellow Ochre for the yellow tulip, Pansy Lavender for the purple tulips, Antique Mauve for the pink tulips and Jade Green for the leaves.

[15] SHADE TULIPS AND LEAVES

All shading and highlighting colors for the tulips and leaves are floated with a side-loaded no. 10 flat/shader. Shade the yellow tulips with Raw Sienna, the pink tulips with Antique Mauve, the purple tulips with Pansy Lavender and the leaves with Plantation Pine.

[16] HIGHLIGHT AND TINT

Highlight all the tulips with Light Buttermilk. Highlight the leaves with a brush mix of Jade Green + Light Buttermilk. To add interest, float tints on the middle of the center tulip petals with side loads on the same brush. Use Antique Mauve on the yellow tulip, Yellow Ochre on the pink tulip and Raw Sienna on the purple tulip.

[17] BASE EGGS

Using a no. 6 filbert, basecoat all the eggs. Use Antique White for the tan egg and a casual mix of Light French Blue + Jade Green + Light Buttermilk for the blue eggs.

[18] SHADE, HIGHLIGHT AND SPECKLE EGGS

All the eggs are shaded and highlighted with side-loaded floats on a no. 10 flat/shader. Shade the tan egg with a brush mix of Raw Sienna + Burnt Umber. Shade the blue egg with a brush mix of Uniform Blue + Plantation Pine. Highlight all the eggs with Light Buttermilk. Speckle the eggs with an 18/0 liner and thinned Burnt Umber.

[19] STROKE IN THE NEST

Load a no. 6 filbert with thinned Mississippi Mud and loosely stroke in the nest. Bring out the rounded shape of the nest by loading Burnt Umber on the dirty brush and swishing the color along the nest bottom and behind the eggs.

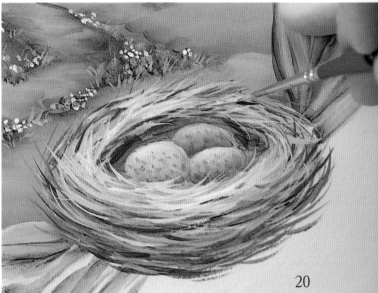

[20] CONTINUE STROKING IN NEST

Make inklike consistency puddles of Burnt Umber, Mississippi Mud, Antique White and Light Buttermilk. Using various colors and mixes, stroke in the nest with an 18/0 script liner. Use a dirty brush as you go from one color to another. Aim for darker colors at the nest bottom and lighter toward the top.

[21] SHADE AND TINT NEST

Using the ½-inch (13mm) flat/wash side-loaded with Burnt Umber, shade along the bottom of the nest and behind the eggs. Then side load with Raw Sienna and float a tint on the right side of the nest.

21

22

[22] PAINT WREATH BRANCHES

Load a no. 1 script liner with thinned Burnt Umber and then pull the brush through thinned Antique White. Paint the wreath, first encircling the heart and then pulling out branches. Using a ¾-inch (19mm) flat/wash and thinned, side-loaded Burnt Umber, shade the background outside of the wreath, near the heart.

[23] PAINT STROKE LEAVES

Now you're ready to paint the stroke leaves (see page 17). Load a no. 8 flat/shader with thinned Light Avocado for leaves outside the wreath. Use Jade Green + Light Buttermilk for leaves inside the wreath. Switch to a no. 4 flat/shader and Plantation Pine to paint the small dark leaves.

[24] PAINT WHITE AND BLUE WREATH FLOWERS

Paint the petals on the white wreath flowers with a no. 4 round stroke and Light Buttermilk. Note that the white petal groupings don't always form a full flower. Using the same brush, load Uniform Blue and tip in Light Buttermilk to paint the petals of the blue flowers. Load a no. 10 flat/shader with Antique Mauve and float the color around the centers of the white flowers. With a no. 2 round stroke, dot the centers of the blue flowers with Yellow Ochre. For the white flower centers, load the brush in Yellow Ochre and tip in Raw Sienna.

23

24

[25] SPATTER BACKGROUND

Cut a sheet of paper roughly to the shape of the wreath and tape it over the wreath. Load an old toothbrush with thinned Burnt Umber and spatter the background (see page 16).

When the painting is dry, finish the surface in the appropriate manner (see pages 10-11).

SPRING WREATH (below)

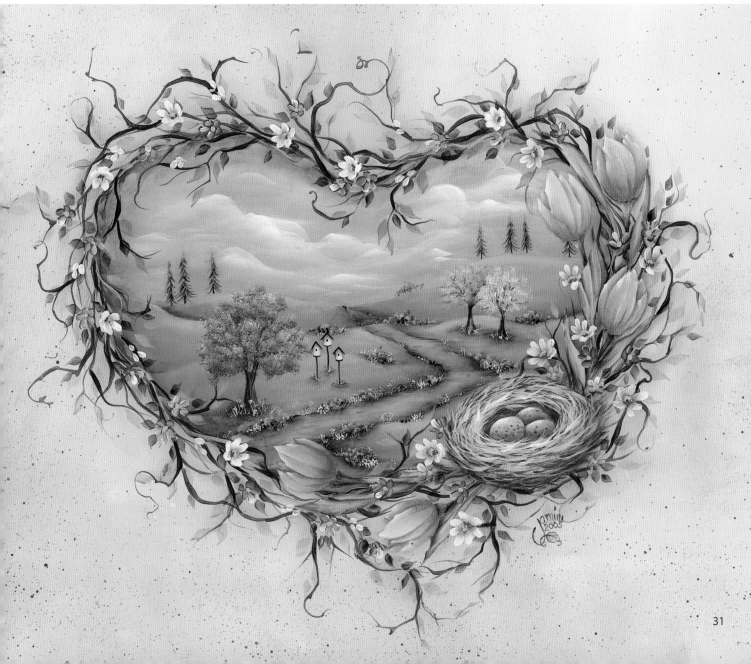

Love Letters

Valentine's Day is the most loving day of the year! These simple "love" letters would make a special gift painted on any surface. Create your own Valentine's Day card for your sweetie, choosing whatever color background you desire. I can also see this design painted on a photo album cover, a special framed plaque or a box.

Materials

LOEW-CORNELL BRUSHES

Flat/wash, series 7550
- ½-inch (13mm)
- ¾-inch (19mm)
- 1-inch (25mm)

Flat/shader, series 7300C
- No. 4
- No. 10

Filbert, series 7500C
- No. 4
- No. 6

Maxine's oval mop, series 270
- ½-inch (13mm)

Liner, series 7350C
- 18/0

Script liner, series 7050
- 18/0

Debbie Mitchell (DM) stippler, series DM
- ⅛-inch (3mm)

Spotter, series 7650
- 3/0

PAINT: DECOART AMERICANA ACRYLICS

Burnt Umber

Fawn

French Grey Blue

French Mauve

Jade Green

Lamp Black

Light Buttermilk

Midnite Green

Mississippi Mud

Rookwood Red

Warm White

Yellow Ochre

ADDITIONAL MATERIALS
- Basics (See list on page 8.)
- Painting surface of your choice, about 8" x 10" (20cm x 25cm)
- Preparation and finishing materials appropriate for your painting surface (See pages 10-11.)

Pattern on page 124.

TRANSFERRING TIP
When transferring a traced design onto the painting surface, place waxed paper over the design. As you press over the pattern lines with your tracing tool, you'll create white lines on the waxed paper, showing what part of the design you've transferred.

[1] PAINT BACKGROUND AND BASE

Prepare your painting surface (see page 10-11). Paint the background Rookwood Red with a 1-inch (25mm) flat/wash. Do all basing with a no. 6 filbert. Use French Mauve for the word *LOVE*, Fawn for the bear, Light Buttermilk for the heart and the envelope and Jade Green for the leaves.

[2] SHADE LETTERS, TINT ENVELOPE AND HEART

Shade letters with Rookwood Red on a ½-inch (13mm) flat/wash and soften with a ½-inch (13mm) mop. Shading goes on the left edges of the letters, especially where they're overlapped by other parts of the painting. Using the same brushes and color, also tint the heart and the envelope.

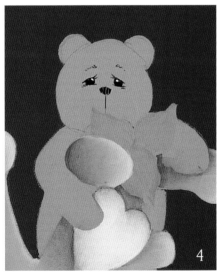

[3] HIGHLIGHT LETTERS

Using the same flat and mop brushes, highlight the letters in Warm White.

[4] PAINT THE BEAR'S FACE

Retrace the bear's face. Paint the eyes, eyebrows, nose and muzzle line in Lamp Black with an 18/0 liner. Highlight the eyes with Warm White on the same brush. Overstroke the nose with lines of Fawn.

[6]
**HIGHLIGHT
BEAR**
Highlight the bear
with a dabby float
of Fawn + Light
Buttermilk on a
no. 10 flat/shader.
Blend with a ½-inch
(13mm) mop.

[5] SHADE BEAR
Shade the bear with a dabby float (see page 13) of Burnt
Umber on a no. 10 flat/shader. Blend with a ½-inch
(13mm) mop. Use shading to create the bear's cheeks.
Let dry and reinforce shadows in the darkest areas.

TEXTURE TIP
When you highlight and
shade the bear, the choppy
motion of the dabby float
gives the fur texture.

**[7] STIPPLE
BRIGHTEST
HIGHLIGHTS**
Tap a dry ⅛-inch
(3mm) DM stippler
on a wet paper
towel. Then pick
up a bit of Light
Buttermilk and tap
in stippling on the
brightest areas of
the highlighting. The
placement can be a
bit hit and miss.

[8] DETAIL TEDDY BEAR'S HEAD

Drybrush scrub (see page 15) the bear's cheeks with Rookwood Red. For the paw lines and muzzle dots, use Burnt Umber on an 18/0 liner. For the hair on the top of the bear's head, use Fawn on the same brush.

[9] SHADE AND HIGHLIGHT ENVELOPE AND HEART

Using a no. 10 flat/shader, shade the heart under the bear's paw with Mississippi Mud. Using the same brush and color, shade the bottom of the envelope and the corner under the *L*. With the same brush, highlight the lower right corner of the envelope and the middle right edge of the heart in Warm White. Blend with the ½-inch (13mm) mop if necessary.

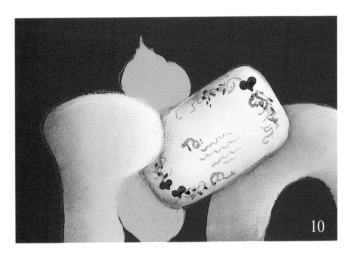

[10] PAINT ENVELOPE DETAILS

For all envelope details, use a 18/0 liner. The lettering is freehanded in Burnt Umber. The vine-like lines are Midnite Green. To form the hearts, dot in two Rookwood Red halves with the liner tip. Then pull the heart's point out with a stylus.

[11] TRIM THE HEART

Using the 18/0 liner and Warm White, outline the heart with scallops. Use a stylus to dot in Rookwood Red at the scallop points.

[12] SHADE, HIGHLIGHT AND TINT LARGE LEAVES

Using a side-loaded no. 10 flat/shader, shade the large leaves with Midnite Green and highlight with Jade Green + Light Buttermilk. Use an 18/0 liner and Midnite Green to paint the leaf veins. Tint here and there on the leaf edges with Rookwood Red sideloaded on a no. 10 flat/shader.

[13] PAINT VINE

To paint the vine, make ink-like consistency puddles of Jade Green and Midnite Green. Load one color on an 18/0 liner and then pull the paint through the second color. Depending on the background, you'll sometimes want the vine darker and sometimes lighter. To make it darker, load in the lighter green first. To make the vine lighter, load in the darker green first. Sometimes the colors will blend to a third color, which is desirable.

[14] PAINT VINE LEAVES

Paint the vine leaves with a no. 4 filbert and the stroke leaf technique (see page 17). Notice that the leaves over the letters are slightly darker so that they'll show up better. The lighter leaves are Jade Green. For the darker leaves, fully load in Midnite Green and then side load in Jade Green.

[15] PAINT THE WHITE FLOWERS

Load an 18/0 liner in Light Buttermilk and stroke in the petals of the white flowers. Tip the brush in Yellow Ochre and dot in centers.

[16] PAINT BLUE FLOWERS

For the blue flowers, use a 3/0 spotter loaded in French Grey Blue and tipped in Warm White. Using the same brush, dot in centers with Yellow Ochre.

1. PAINT FIRST C-STROKE
Begin your rose or bud with a C-stroke to start the formation of the rose's bowl.

2. PAINT SECOND C-STROKE
Finish the bowl with a second C-stroke painted upside down and fitted over the first. For buds, stop here.

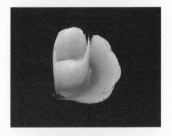

3. ADD SHRIMP STROKE
Begin the rose skirt by adding a shrimp-stroke outer petal.

4. CONTINUE
Add another one or two shrimp strokes to complete the rose.

[17] PAINT THE ROSES

Paint the roses and buds with a no. 4 flat/shader. Load in French Mauve and then side load one side in Rookwood Red and the other side in Warm White. Blend on the palette. The bowl of the roses and the rose buds are formed with two C-strokes (see page 16). The outer rose petals are shrimp strokes (see page 17). "Assembling a Rose" on this page shows how the strokes fit together.

Repeat the strokes as needed to define the petals. Then clean the brush and side load Warm White to redefine the roses and buds with highlights on the petal edges and at the top of the bowl. Dot inside the bowl of the big roses with Rookwood Red and with Warm White on an 18/0 liner. Use a 3/0 spotter loaded in Jade Green to paint the sepals.

The rose in the valentine is painted the same way as the roses on the vine. The stem and leaves are also painted with the same colors and techniques as those on the vine (see steps 13 and 14), but with a no. 4 flat/shader for the leaves.

[18] FLOAT AND STROKE THE GRASS

Using a ¾-inch (19mm) flat/wash, float Jade Green into the grassy area. Then use the 18/0 script liner to stroke grasses in Jade Green, Light Buttermilk and Midnite Green. Use a dirty brush as you move from one grass color to another.

When the painting is dry, finish the surface in the appropriate manner (see pages 10-11).

LOVE LETTERS (below)

Lucky Leprechaun

This impish little fellow tucked among the shamrocks is protecting his pot o' gold!
Paint him on a plate for display or on a shirt to wear on the seventeenth of March.
For an alternate background, try a soft ivory color, floating blue for the sky area and
a bit of green under the pot to set it off.

Materials

LOEW-CORNELL BRUSHES

Flat/wash, series 7550
- ½-inch (13mm)
- ¾-inch (19mm)
- 1-inch (25mm)

Flat/shader, series 7300C
- No. 10

Filbert, series 7500C
- No. 4
- No. 6

Liner, series 7350C
- 10/0

Script liner, series 7050
- 18/0

Round, series 7000
- No. 1

Debbie Mitchell (DM) stippler, series DM
- ¼-inch (6mm)

ADDITIONAL MATERIALS
- Basics (See list on page 8.)
- Painting surface of your choice, about 8" x 10" (20cm x 25cm)
- Preparation and finishing materials appropriate for your painting surface (See pages 10-11.)

Pattern on page 124.

PAINT: DECOART AMERICANA ACRYLICS

Antique Mauve

Dusty Rose

Evergreen

French Grey Blue

Golden Straw

Hauser Light Green

Honey Brown

Lamp Black

Light Avocado

Light Buttermilk

Milk Chocolate

Neutral Grey

Traditional Burnt Sienna

Uniform Blue

BRUSH CARE TIP
Never let your brushes sit in the water basin for long periods of time. If you do, the hairs will distort. For the same reason, make sure you store your brushes with the hairs pointing upward.

[1] PAINT BACKGROUND AND BASE

Prepare your painting surface (see pages 10-11). Paint the background with a 1-inch (25mm) flat/wash and French Grey Blue + a touch of Light Buttermilk. Slip-slap the color on the painting surface. Shade around the design with a ¾-inch (19mm) flat/wash side-loaded with Uniform Blue.

Using a no. 4 filbert, base the leprechaun's face with Dusty Rose, the shoes, hands, belt and hat with Lamp Black, the trousers, vest and hatband with Light Avocado and the shirtsleeves with Light Buttermilk. Base the pot with a no. 6 filbert and Lamp Black, switching to a 10/0 liner for the handles. Returning to a no. 6 filbert, base the gold in the pot with Honey Brown tipped in Golden Straw and the shamrocks with Light Avocado. Base the buckle with a no. 1 round and Honey Brown.

[2] SHADE AND HIGHLIGHT GREEN CLOTHING

Shade the leprechaun's trousers, vest and hatband with a no. 10 flat/shader and side-loaded Evergreen. With the same brush, highlight with side-loaded Hauser Light Green. Float the highlight on the vest and create a bull's-eye float (see page 14) on the trousers. Use a side-by-side float (see page 14) to highlight the hatband.

[3] ADD DETAILS

Stripe the vest with an 18/0 script liner and Hauser Light Green. Stripe the pants with the same brush and Evergreen. Dot the vest buttons and the hatband spots with Lamp Black on a stylus.

SHADING TIP

If you're not sure where to float shading, refer to the pattern's shading dot and lines. The darker the lines and dots, the darker the shading, although these markings are just suggestions.

[4] HIGHLIGHT AND SHADE REMAINING CLOTHING

Highlight the hat, belt, gloves and shoes with a 10 flat/shader side-loaded with Neutral Grey. The hat highlight is a side-by-side float. Shade the shirt with a no. 10 flat/shader and side-loaded Neutral Grey. Highlight the belt buckle with a dry no. 1 round and Golden Straw.

[5] START THE LEPRECHAUN'S FACE

Transfer the pattern lines for the leprechaun's face and the shamrocks on the pot. Paint the leprechaun's eyebrows, eyes, mouth, cheek line and lip line with a 10/0 liner and Lamp Black. Use the same brush to fill in the nose with a wash of Antique Mauve. Highlight the eyes with Light Buttermilk on the tip of the liner. Shade at the top of the head, where the ears meet the face, under the nose and under the mouth with a no. 10 flat/shader and Traditional Burnt Sienna + Dusty Rose.

[6] FINISH THE LEPRECHAUN'S FACE

Highlight the top of the nose, along the ear line and the bottom of the face with a no. 10 flat/shader side-loaded with Light Buttermilk. Float the lip with Antique Mauve loaded on the same brush. Drybrush scrub (see page 15) the cheeks with a ¼-inch (6mm) DM stippler and Antique Mauve.

[7] STROKE IN HAIR AND BEARD

Stroke in the hair and beard with an 18/0 script liner, going in and out of Traditional Burnt Sienna and Dusty Rose.

[8] SHADE GOLD, ADD CONTOUR AND RUST TO POT

Shade the gold under the leprechaun, using the ½-inch (13mm) flat/wash and Milk Chocolate. Side load the same brush in Neutral Grey and apply a dabby float (see page 13) along the bottom of the pot and the ball feet. Walk the color upwards into the pot. Using the same brush side-loaded with a brush mix of Neutral Grey + Traditional Burnt Sienna, apply bull's-eye floats to create rust effects here and there on the pot surface.

[9] PAINT DESIGN ON POT

Paint the shamrock detail on the pot using the 10/0 liner and thinned Hauser Light Green. With the stylus add dots of Hauser Light Green here and there. Using the no. 1 round and Neutral Grey add strokes along the top edge of the pot.

MOISTENING TIP

Moisten a large area on a paper towel. When you feel the need for just a bit more wetness in your brush, simply stroke the brush across this moist area.

[10] PAINT THE OTHER SHAMROCKS

Paint all the "real" shamrocks (those not part of the pot design) in the following manner: Shade with a ½-inch (13mm) flat/wash side-loaded in Evergreen. Highlight with Hauser Light Green. Paint the linework with an 18/0 script liner and thinned Hauser Light Green.

[11] FLOAT AND STROKE IN GRASS

Float the ground area with a side load of Hauser Light Green on a ¾-inch (19mm) flat/wash. Stroke in the grass with an 18/0 script liner, working in and out of thinned Evergreen and Hauser Light Green.

When the painting is dry, finish the surface in the appropriate manner (see pages 10-11).

LUCKY LEPRECHAUN (below)

45

Bunny Takes a Breather

To help celebrate Easter, this dear bunny could be painted on a basket lid, a wall plaque, a shirt or any number of other surfaces. Quick-and-easy stroke flowers surround the area where the bunny is napping. You could use these flowers as a border for an entirely different design. The eggs are also simple to paint. Have fun experimenting with the colors on your palette. Decorate the eggs as you might have when you were a kid!

Materials

LOEW-CORNELL BRUSHES

Flat/wash, series 7550
- ½-inch (13mm)
- ¾-inch (19mm)
- 1-inch (25mm)

Flat/shader, series 7300C
- No. 2
- No. 6
- No. 10

Filbert, series 7500C
- No. 6

Liner, series 7350C
- 18/0
- 10/0

Script liner
- 18/0

Round, series 7000
- No. 1

Round stroke, series 7040
- No. 2
- No. 4

Debbie Mitchell (DM) stippler, series DM
- ¼-inch (6mm)

ADDITIONAL MATERIALS

- Basics (See list on page 8.)
- Painting surface of your choice, about 9" x 11" (23cm x 28cm)
- Preparation and finishing materials appropriate for your painting surface (See pages 10-11.)

Pattern on page 124.

PAINT: DECOART AMERICANA ACRYLICS

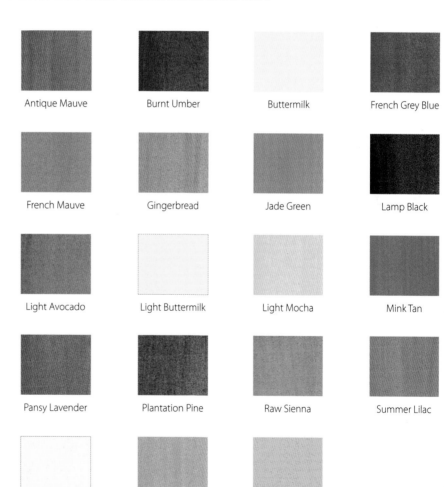

Antique Mauve	Burnt Umber	Buttermilk	French Grey Blue
French Mauve	Gingerbread	Jade Green	Lamp Black
Light Avocado	Light Buttermilk	Light Mocha	Mink Tan
Pansy Lavender	Plantation Pine	Raw Sienna	Summer Lilac
Warm White	Winter Blue	Yellow Ochre	

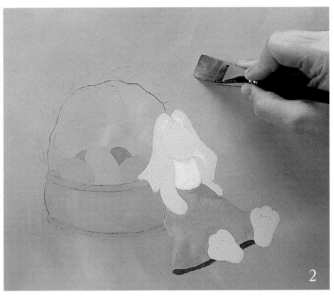

[1] PAINT BACKGROUND AND BASECOAT

Prepare your painting surface (see pages 10-11). Paint the background Jade Green + Light Buttermilk, slip-slapping in the color with a 1-inch (25mm) flat/wash. Using a no. 6 filbert, base the bunny with Light Mocha, the bodice with Light Buttermilk and the dress with slip-slapped Summer Lilac + Buttermilk. With the same brush, base the eggs in Jade Green, Summer Lilac, Winter Blue, French Mauve and Yellow Ochre (one color per egg). Refer to the finished painting on page 46 for placement of the colors. Base the underside of the skirt bottom with Pansy Lavender on a no. 2 round stroke. Wash over the basket with a ½-inch (13mm) flat/wash and Mink Tan.

[2] FLOAT IN THE SKY

To paint the sky around the top of the basket and under the handle, side load Winter Blue onto a ¾-inch (19mm) flat/wash and apply bull's-eye floats (see page 14).

[3] ADD CLOUDS

For the clouds, side load a ¾-inch (19mm) flat/wash in scant Light Buttermilk. Make arched strokes for the puffiness of the clouds and then flatten out the bottoms of the clouds.

[4] PAINT INSIDE OF EARS, SHADE AND HIGHLIGHT BUNNY

Load a no. 2 round stroke with Antique Mauve and paint the inside of the ears. With a ½-inch (13mm) flat/wash, shade the bunny in Mink Tan + Burnt Umber. Highlight with Light Buttermilk. Note that the shading and highlighting help to create the fold in the left ear and to separate the toes.

[5] FLOAT MORE SHADING

With the no. 10 flat/shader and Antique Mauve, float more shading under the toes and inside the ears.

[6] PAINT THE FACE

Transfer the pattern lines for the facial features and the heart on the bodice. Paint the eyelashes, the inside of the mouth and the lip line under the mouth with Lamp Black and an 18/0 liner. With the same brush, paint the eyebrows and the line connecting the nose and mouth with Burnt Umber. Still with the 18/0 liner, fill in the nose with a wash of Antique Mauve. Shade the side of the nose line and above the eyelashes with Burnt Umber + Mink Tan on a no. 10 flat/shader. Highlight above the nose with Light Buttermilk.

FACIAL EXPRESSION TIP

If you prefer your bunny bright-eyed and bushy-tailed (so to speak) then paint her with open eyes. You can freehand them or use the eyes from "Lucky Leprechaun" (page 40) or the gingerbread girl in "Snowy Tree" (page 116) as a guide. Slightly altering facial features creates a whole new expression. Give it a try!

[7] ADD HAIR, WHISKERS AND FACE DETAILS

Using the 18/0 script liner and Warm White, pull whiskers from the nose outward. Paint the hair with an 18/0 script liner and Burnt Umber tipped in Light Buttermilk. Float the lower lip with a no. 6 flat/shader and Antique Mauve. With the ¼-inch (6mm) DM stippler and Antique Mauve, use a drybrush scrub (see page 15) to add a bit of cheek color.

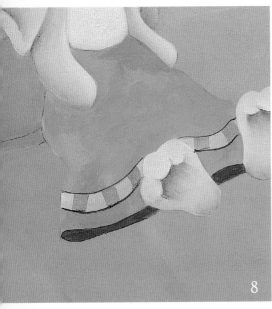

[8] PAINT SKIRT STRIPE

Paint the stripe on the skirt bottom with Light Buttermilk on a no. 6 flat/shader. Add checks on the stripe with water-thinned Plantation Pine. Using the same color, line the top and bottom of the stripe with an 18/0 script liner.

[9] SHADE AND HIGHLIGHT SKIRT

Using a ½-inch (13mm) flat/wash, shade the skirt with Pansy Lavender + a touch of Lamp Black. Shade the underskirt with the same brush and colors, but add more Lamp Black to the mix. Highlight the skirt with side-loaded Warm White. After highlighting, soften the edges by pulling down with the water corner of the brush. Note how the shading and highlighting create the skirt gathers.

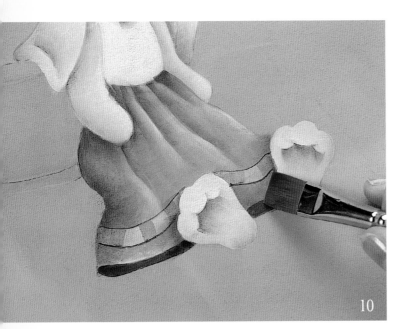

[10] TINT THE SKIRT

Tint the left side of the skirt and along the skirt hem with Antique Mauve side-loaded on a ½-inch (13mm) flat/wash.

[11] SHADE AND HIGHLIGHT BODICE, ADD BUTTONS

Using a ½-inch (13mm) flat/wash, side load Mink Tan to shade the bodice. Then side load Warm White for the highlighting. Use a stylus to dot on Pansy Lavender buttons.

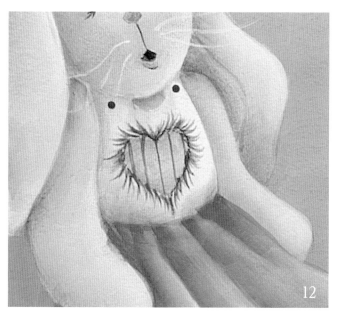

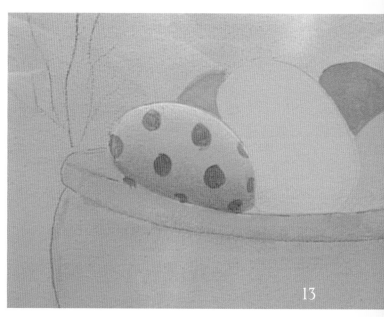

[12] DETAIL THE HEART AND TINT

Using an 18/0 liner and inklike consistency Burnt Umber, stroke in the twig heart and pull a line along the neckline. Using the same brush, stripe the heart with Pansy Lavender. Side load a no. 10 flat/shader with Pansy Lavender and float a tint at the top of the heart and the bottom left of the bodice. Side load the same brush with Light Avocado and float in a tint at the bottom of the heart and on the bottom right of the bodice.

[13] DECORATE THE PINK EGG

You can either freehand the egg designs or transfer the pattern lines. Paint the dots on the pink egg with a no. 1 round. Shade the pink egg with Antique Mauve side-loaded on a ½-inch (13mm) flat/wash. Highlight with Warm White and the same brush.

[14] DECORATE THE YELLOW EGG

Using a no. 2 flat/shader, stripe the yellow egg with Gingerbread. Use a ½-inch (13mm) flat/wash side-loaded with Raw Sienna to shade. Highlight with the same brush and side-loaded Warm White. Add Raw Sienna stylus dots.

[15] DECORATE THE BLUE EGG

Using a no. 6 flat/shader, stripe the blue egg with Warm White. Use a ½-inch (13mm) flat/wash side-loaded with French Grey Blue to shade. Highlight with the same brush and side-loaded Warm White. Add Warm White stylus dots.

[16] DECORATE GREEN AND PURPLE EGGS

Add Plantation Pine stylus dots to the green egg. Use a no. 10 flat/shader side-loaded with Plantation Pine to shade. Use a 10/0 liner to paint the wavy lines and the dots on the purple egg. Use a no. 10 flat/shader side-loaded with Pansy Lavender + a touch of Lamp Black to shade. Then highlight both eggs with a no. 10 flat/shader side-loaded with Warm White.

[17] WEAVE THE BASKET

Using a no. 4 round stroke and thinned Burnt Umber, paint the basket weavings. To do so, touch down, press and lift, repeating the process in rows across the basket. Note that the thick and thin portions of the weavings are staggered from one row to the next.

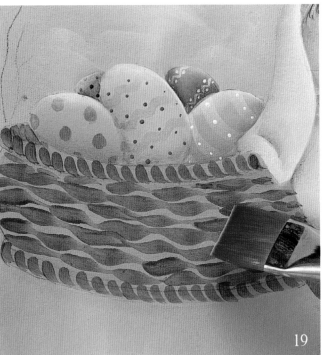

[18] PAINT BASKET RIM

Using the same brush and color, paint the top and bottom basket rims in a series of short strokes.

[19] APPLY WASH

Using a ¾-inch (19mm) flat/wash, brush lightly over the basket and rims with thinned Raw Sienna.

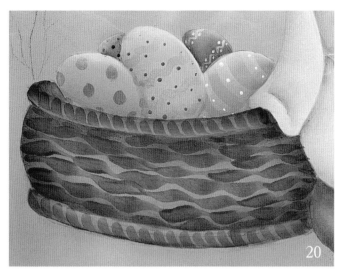

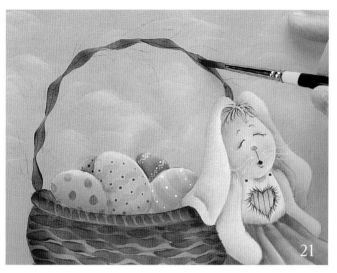

[20] SHADE AND HIGHLIGHT BASKET

Using a ¾-inch (19mm) flat/wash and side-loaded thinned Burnt Umber + a touch of Lamp Black, shade both sides of the basket, beneath the top rim and above the bottom rim. Switch to a no. 10 flat/shader and, with the same side-loaded color, shade the top of the top rim and the bottom of the bottom rim. Side load the same brush with thinned Yellow Ochre + Raw Sienna and highlight the bottom of the top rim and the top of the bottom rim.

[21] PAINT BASKET HANDLE

Paint the basket handle with a no. 4 round stroke and Burnt Umber, using the same technique used for the basket weavings in step 17.

[22] PAINT THE VINE

Pull off vines with an 18/0 script liner. Add stroke leaves (see page 17) with a no. 6 flat/shader loaded in thinned Plantation Pine.

[23] ADD THE RIBBON

Paint the ribbon with a no. 2 round stroke loaded with thinned Pansy Lavender and tipped with Buttermilk.

[24] BASE AND HIGHLIGHT GRASS

With a ¾-inch (19mm) flat/wash, float thinned Plantation Pine in the grass area. Go for a washy, watercolor effect. With the dirty brush, stroke in highlights with Jade Green + a touch of Light Buttermilk.

[25] PULL GRASS BLADES AND STEMS

Load an 18/0 liner with Plantation Pine and pull in grass blades. Using the dirty brush, switch to Jade Green for the blades that overlap the basket and the dress. The lighter color in these areas is needed for contrast. For the bouquet stems, switch to an 18/0 script liner loaded in Plantation Pine and tipped in Jade Green.

[26] PAINT LEAVES AND RIBBON

Load a no. 2 round stroke with Plantation Pine, tip in Jade Green and add stroke leaves (see page 17) on bouquet and ground flowers. Pull in the bouquet ribbon with an 18/0 script liner loaded in Warm White.

[27] ADD THE RIBBON

Paint the ribbon with thinned Pansy Lavender on a no. 2 round stroke tipped with Buttermilk.

[28] PAINT PINK FLOWERS

Stroke in the pink flowers with an 18/0 liner loaded with Antique Mauve and tipped in Light Buttermilk. Use the brush tip to dot in Yellow Ochre centers.

When the painting is completely dry, finish the surface in the appropriate manner (see pages 10-11).

BUNNY TAKES A BREATHER (below)

Summer Wreath

AS SPRING TURNS TO SUMMER, the days begin to shine with rich golden tones. Lush gardens and beautiful wildflowers abound, and we look forward to those lazy days spent soaking up the sun.

In this painting, the light and dark greens of early summer show up in the vegetation of the fields and pastures. By adding a bit more yellow or gold to your brush, you can create a late summer appearance. The white daisies on the wreath can be changed dramatically by pulling the shading color out wider on the petals or by tinting one side of the flower with a blue or lavender. Experiment! You can make this painting your own by altering a few subtle touches.

Materials

LOEW-CORNELL BRUSHES

Flat/wash, series 7550
- ½-inch (13mm)
- ¾-inch (19mm)
- 1-inch (25mm)

Flat/shader, series 7300C
- No. 8
- No. 10

Filbert, series 7500C
- No. 6
- No. 8
- No. 10

Liner, series 7350C
- 18/0

Script liner, series 7050
- 18/0
- No. 1

Round Stroke, series 7040
- No. 2
- No. 4

Debbie Mitchell (DM) stippler, series DM
- ⅛-inch (3mm)
- ⅜-inch (10mm)
- ½-inch (13mm)

Crescent, series 247
- ⅜-inch (10mm)

ADDITIONAL MATERIALS

- Basics (See list on page 8.)
- Painting surface of your choice, about 12" x 16" (31cm x 41cm)
- Preparation and finishing materials appropriate for your painting surface (See pages 10-11.)
- Spattering materials: toothbrush and paper to cover painting.

Pattern on page 122.

PAINT: DECOART AMERICANA ACRYLICS

Antique Mauve

Antique White

Burnt Orange

Burnt Umber

Fawn

Golden Straw

Hauser Light Green

Jade Green

Lamp Black

Light Avocado

Light Buttermilk

Light French Blue

Midnite Green

Mississippi Mud

Plantation Pine

Raw Sienna

Rookwood Red

Traditional Burnt Sienna

Uniform Blue

Warm White

Yellow Ochre

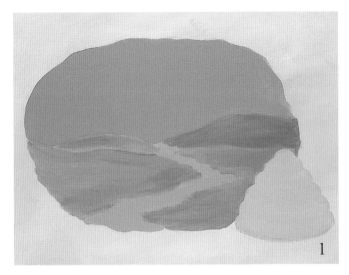

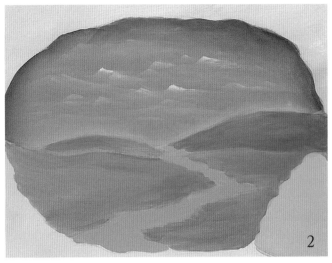

[1] PREPARE, TRACE AND BASE

Prepare your painting surface (see pages 10-11). Paint the background in a slip-slap manner with a 1-inch (25mm) flat/wash double-loaded with Antique White and Light Buttermilk. Let dry. Transfer the wreath inset and the outline onto the surface. Using a no. 10 filbert, base the sky with Light French Blue, the grassy areas with Light Avocado + a touch of Jade Green and a little Golden Straw on the dirty brush, and the brown hill in the back with Mississippi Mud + Antique White + Light Avocado. Using a no. 8 filbert, base the path with Fawn and the beehive with Yellow Ochre.

[2] ENHANCE SKY

Side load a ¾-inch (19mm) flat/wash with Light French Blue + Light Buttermilk and float along the horizon line. Side load the same brush with Light Buttermilk. Touch the chisel and skip along to create clouds. Then smear the bottoms a bit with the water side of the brush. Shade the top of the sky with the same brush side-loaded in Uniform Blue.

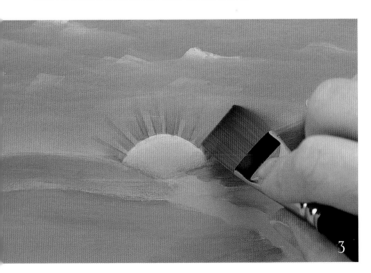

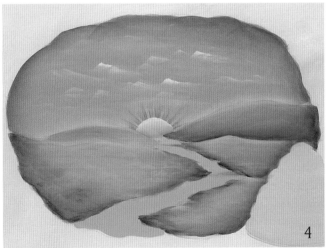

[3] PAINT THE SUN

Base the sun with a no. 6 filbert and Yellow Ochre. Shade the bottom with a ½-inch (13mm) flat/wash side-loaded with Raw Sienna. With the same brush, side load Light Buttermilk and highlight the top of the sun. Use a ¾-inch (19mm) flat/wash side-loaded with Yellow Ochre to float an "aura" around the sun. Side load the same brush with Raw Sienna and paint the sun's rays with a stutter float (see page 13).

[4] SHADE AND HIGHLIGHT GREEN HILLS

Side load a ¾-inch (19mm) flat/wash with a brush mix of Plantation Pine and Light Avocado and shade the green hills. Deepen the shading with Plantation Pine. Highlight the hills with a brush mix of Light Avocado + Yellow Ochre. Brighten the highlight with Golden Straw.

[5] SHADE AND HIGHLIGHT BROWN HILL

Using dark graphite paper, transfer the pattern of the crop rows, trees, birdhouses and beehives. Then shade the brown hill with Burnt Umber side-loaded on a ½-inch (13mm) flat/wash. Highlight the top of the brown hill with Yellow Ochre side-loaded on the same brush.

[6] TAP IN CROP ROWS

With a no. 2 round stroke loaded in Plantation Pine and tipped in Jade Green, tap in the crop rows on the back hills. Float shadows on both sides of each row with a side-loaded no. 8 flat/shader, using Burnt Umber on the left hill and Plantation Pine on the right.

[7] SHADE, HIGHLIGHT AND TINT ROAD

Using a ½-inch (13mm) flat/wash, shade the path with dabby floats (see page 13) of side-loaded Burnt Umber. Using the same brush, add dabby Yellow Ochre highlights along the middle area of the road. Then tint the road edges here and there with side-loaded Plantation Pine and also with side-loaded Yellow Ochre. Walk the tints out a bit.

[8] PAINT TRUNKS AND BRANCHES

Paint all deciduous tree trunks and branches with a no. 2 round stroke loaded in Burnt Umber and tipped in Lamp Black. Then tip the dirty brush in Fawn and add a few highlights.

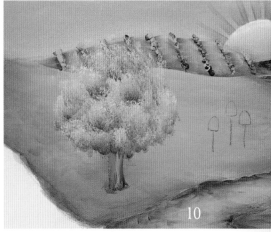

[9] PAINT FOLIAGE ON SMALL TREES

To paint the foliage on the small trees to the right, moisten a ½-inch (13mm) DM stippler and double load with Hauser Light Green and Plantation Pine. Tap the brush on the palette to blend. Then tip in Light Buttermilk and tap to blend again. Stipple the foliage. For the highlights, load the dirty brush with Yellow Ochre, tap on the palette and then stipple. Separate the trees and shade the bottom of the foliage with a float of Plantation Pine side-loaded on a ½-inch (13mm) flat/wash.

[10] PAINT FOLIAGE ON LARGE TREE

For the foliage on the large tree, moisten a ⅜-inch (10mm) DM stippler and double load with Jade Green and Plantation Pine. Tap the brush on the palette to blend. Then tip in Light Buttermilk and tap to blend again. Stipple the foliage. For the highlights, load the dirty brush in Yellow Ochre, tap on the palette and then stipple. Shade the bottom of the foliage with a float of Plantation Pine side-loaded on a ½-inch (13mm) flat/wash.

[11] PAINT FIRS

Using an 18/0 liner and Burnt Umber, paint the fir trunks. Load the same brush in Plantation Pine and stroke in the branches. Then tip the dirty brush in Jade Green and overstroke the branches.

[12] PAINT TINY BEEHIVES

Paint the posts of the three beehives next to the road with Burnt Umber on an 18/0 liner. Using the same brush, base the hives in Yellow Ochre. Dot the openings and pull the lines under the hives with Burnt Umber. With a no. 8 flat/shader, shade the tops of the hives with side-loaded Raw Sienna + Traditional Burnt Sienna.

13

14

[13] STIPPLE IN BUSHES

Double load a moistened ⅛-inch (3mm) DM stippler with Plantation Pine and Yellow Ochre and stipple in bushes here and there along the path and against the back hills.

[14] DOT IN FLOWERS AND ADD GRASSES

Dot in flowers along the path and under the trees with an 18/0 liner. Use Burnt Orange tipped in Yellow Ochre, Rookwood Red tipped in Antique White, Yellow Ochre tipped in Light Buttermilk, and Uniform Blue tipped in Light French Blue and Light Buttermilk.

In order to ground the three beehives, the two small trees and the little mound of flowers to the right of the three beehives side load a no. 10 flat/shader with Plantation Pine and float some darker grass under them. Load the same color on an 18/0 liner and pull a few grasses in the same areas and along the path here and there.

15

[15] START BEEHIVE

Load an 18/0 liner with Raw Sienna and pull the horizontal and vertical lines on the large beehive. With the same brush, fill in the hole under the beehive handle with Light Avocado. Paint the opening to the beehive with a no. 2 round stroke and Burnt Umber. If necessary, clean up the outer edges of the beehive with the same brush and Yellow Ochre. Then take a ¾-inch (19mm) flat/wash side-loaded with Raw Sienna + Burnt Umber and float shading on the left and right sides of the beehive.

16

[16] SHADE BEEHIVE LINES

Load Raw Sienna + Burnt Umber on a ½-inch (13mm) flat/wash and shade the beehive separation lines. This shading is applied to both sides of the vertical lines and right above the horizontal lines.

[17] STUTTER FLOAT

With the same brush and colors, stutter float (see page 13) shading along the vertical lines to create texture.

[18] HIGHLIGHT, TINT AND SHADE HIVE

Load a ⅜-inch (10mm) dry crescent brush with Light Buttermilk and scrub highlighting on the beehive sections, staying lightest in the middle of the hive. Keep your brush parallel to the horizontal lines. Paint over the vertical separation lines with an 18/0 script liner and Yellow Ochre. Side load a ¾-inch (19mm) flat/wash with Traditional Burnt Sienna and tint the outer edges of both sides of the hive. Then take a no. 10 flat/shader and shade the right side of the hive opening with side-loaded Burnt Umber.

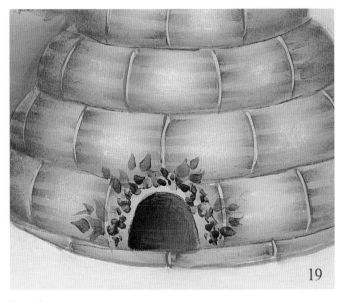

[19] ARCH LEAVES OVER OPENING

Load a no. 2 round stroke with Plantation Pine, tip in Jade Green and stipple in greenery around the beehive opening. Then add individual leaves with Plantation Pine and the no. 2 round stroke.

[20] PAINT VINE BRANCHES

Side load a 1-inch (25mm) flat/wash with Mississippi Mud and float around the scene. Begin the vine wreath with a no. 4 round stroke loaded with thinned Raw Sienna and then run through thinned Burnt Umber. Load a no. 2 round stroke with thinned Raw Sienna and drag the brush through thinned Light Buttermilk and pull in some vines over the sky and grass. Also add highlights here and there along the Raw Sienna + Burnt Umber vine and pull a few curlicues. Side load a ¾-inch (19mm) flat/wash with Burnt Umber and float some color along the vines here and there to give them depth.

[21] PAINT LEAVES AND GREEN VINES

Load a no. 10 filbert with thinned Light Avocado, side load with Midnite Green and add stroke leaves (see page 17) on the wreath. Load a ⅜-inch (10mm) DM stippler with Plantation Pine and tap on the palette. Then load the other brush side with Jade Green and tap the palette again. Stipple color in the area around the beehive. Pull the green vines with a no. 1 script liner and Plantation Pine + Jade Green. Add a bit of Light Buttermilk to the vines overlapping the sky and the grass.

[22] PULL GRASSES UNDER HIVE

Side load a ¾-inch (19mm) flat/wash with Plantation Pine and shade beneath the beehive. Load an 18/0 script liner with Jade Green + Plantation Pine and pull up a few grass blades beneath the beehive.

[23] PAINT DAISY PETALS

Stroke in the large daisy petals with a no. 10 filbert and Warm White. You may have to repaint the petals to make them more opaque. Side load Antique Mauve on a ½-inch (13mm) flat/wash and, moving around the flower centers, randomly tint some of the petals. Also tint with Raw Sienna and Plantation Pine. Some of the tints can overlap each other.

[24] PAINT DAISY CENTERS, ADD LEAVES

Double load a ⅛-inch (3mm) stippler with Golden Straw and Light Buttermilk and tap in the daisy centers. Shade the centers with a no. 10 flat/shader side-loaded with Raw Sienna + Traditional Burnt Sienna. Add more leaves in the sky area and green areas of the vine with a no. 10 filbert double-loaded with Plantation Pine and Jade Green + Light Buttermilk.

[25] PAINT FILLER FLOWERS AND SPATTER

Use a no. 4 round stroke and Light Buttermilk for the petals of the white filler flowers. Paint the centers in Raw Sienna tipped in Golden Straw. The colored filler flowers are painted with a no. 2 round stroke. Make some with petals of Burnt Orange tipped in Yellow Ochre and centers of Rookwood Red. Make some with petals of Rookwood Red tipped with Antique Mauve and centers of Yellow Ochre. Make still others with petals of Light Buttermilk and centers of Burnt Umber.

Cut a sheet of paper roughly to the shape of the wreath and tape it over the wreath. Load an old toothbrush with thinned Burnt Umber and spatter the background (see page 16).

When the painting is completely dry, finish the surface in the appropriate manner (see pages 10-11).

SUMMER WREATH (below)

25

Americana

Materials

LOEW-CORNELL BRUSHES

Flat/wash, series 7550
- ½-inch (13mm)
- ¾-inch (19mm)
- 1-inch (25mm)

Flat/shader, series 7300C
- No. 2
- No. 6
- No. 8
- No. 10

Filbert, series 7500C
- No. 6

Maxine's oval mop, series 270
- 3⁄4-inch (19mm)

Liner, series 7350C
- 18/0
- No. 0

Round, series 7000
- No. 1

Debbie Mitchell (DM) stippler, series DM
- ¼-inch (6mm)

ADDITIONAL MATERIALS
- Basics (See list on page 8.)
- Painting surface of your choice, about 11" x 9" (28cm x 23cm)
- Preparation and finishing materials appropriate for your painting surface (See pages 10-11.)
- American Traditional Stencils brass template MS-121 (stars, hearts and dots)

Pattern on page 124.

Celebrate the Fourth of July by painting this patriotic design on a wall plaque, or perhaps a memory album cover personalized for a loved one. You can omit any element—maybe the doll or watermelon—and add more sunflowers peeking around the flag. The trailing vines and leaves through the design help fill blank areas while adding interest and a touch of nature.

PAINT: DECOART AMERICANA ACRYLICS

Burnt Umber

Buttermilk

Deep Midnight Blue

Dusty Rose

Fawn

Lamp Black

Light Avocado

Light Buttermilk

Mississippi Mud

Plantation Pine

Raw Sienna

Rookwood Red

Traditional Burnt Sienna

Warm White

Yellow Ochre

FLOATING TIP
Let your floats for shading, highlighting and glazing dry well between layers. You can accelerate the drying time with a hair dryer.

[1] PAINT BACKGROUND AND BASECOAT

Prepare your painting surface (see pages 10-11). Paint background in Buttermilk with a 1-inch (25mm) flat/wash. Using a ½-inch (13mm) flat/wash, base the union (blue part) of the large "flag" in washy Deep Midnight Blue and the red stripes in washy Rookwood Red. Leave the white stripes the background color. Use the same colors for the doll's flag, but switch to a no. 1 round. Base the hearts with a no. 6 filbert and Light Buttermilk. Base the birdhouse with the same brush, using washy Fawn for the walls and washy Burnt Umber for the roof. Still using the no. 6 filbert, base the doll's face with washy Dusty Rose and the shoes with washy Lamp Black. Base the flagpole with a no. 1 round and washy Burnt Umber. The ball on top of the flagpole is washy Raw Sienna. Base the sunflower and watermelon with a no. 6 filbert. Use thinned Light Avocado for the watermelon rind and slip-slapped Rookwood Red + Light Buttermilk for the inside. Base the sun flower petals in a wash of Yellow Ochre, the center in a dabby wash of Raw Sienna and the leaves in a wash of Light Avocado.

[2] SHADE AROUND DESIGN

Shade around the design with a ¾-inch (19mm) flat/wash side-loaded with Mississippi Mud. Soften with a ¾-inch (19mm) oval mop.

[3] STENCIL STARS

Using a slightly damp ¼-inch (6mm) DM Stippler and Warm White, stencil stars in the union (blue) portion of the large "flag."

[4] SHADE AND HIGHLIGHT UNION, PAINT CHECKS

Shade around the inside edge of the union and above and below the hearts with a ½-inch (13mm) flat/wash side-loaded with Deep Midnight Blue. Drybrush highlight through the open areas with a ¼-inch (6mm) DM stippler and Warm White. Paint the union checks with a no. 6 flat/shader and Deep Midnight Blue.

5

6

[5] SHADE AND HIGHLIGHT STRIPES

Using a side-loaded ½-inch (13mm) flat/wash, shade the red stripes in Rookwood Red and the white stripes in Mississippi Mud. Drybrush highlight the middle area of both the red and white stripes with a ¼-inch (6mm) DM stippler and Warm White.

[6] PLAID AND DOT THE STRIPES

Paint the plaid on the red strips with a no. 8 flat/shader and very thin Rookwood Red. Add dots to the white stripes with Mississippi Mud on a stylus.

7

8

[7] TINT HEARTS AND STENCIL STARS

Tint the hearts in the union with a ½-inch (13mm) side-loaded flat/wash. To do this, float Mississippi Mud at the tops of all the hearts. Then float Rookwood Red at the bottom of the left heart, Warm White at the bottom of the middle heart and Deep Midnight Blue at the bottom of the right heart.

Drybrush stencil the stars in the middle of the hearts with a ¼-inch (6mm) DM stippler. Use Rookwood Red for the left star, Mississippi Mud for the center star and Deep Midnight Blue for the right star.

[8] LINE AND STITCH

Using an 18/0 liner and Lamp Black, line and "stitch" around the union and the stripes. Also paint stitching around the hearts.

[9] PAINT SUNFLOWER

Shade and highlight the sunflower blossom and leaves with a side-loaded no. 10 flat/shader. Shade the petals and the flower center with Raw Sienna. Deepen this shading with Traditional Burnt Sienna + Burnt Umber. Highlight the very middle of the sunflower and the petal ends with dabby floats (see page 13) of Yellow Ochre + Light Buttermilk. Shade the sunflower leaves with Plantation Pine and highlight with Yellow Ochre.

Line the sunflower petals and leaves with an 18/0 liner. Use Plantation Pine around the leaves and Raw Sienna around the petals. Use a stylus to dot Lamp Black around the center of the sunflower.

[10] SHADE AND HIGHLIGHT BIRDHOUSE

Shade and highlight the birdhouse with a side-loaded ½-inch (13mm) flat/wash. Shade the house with Mississippi Mud and then deepen with Burnt Umber. Also use the same color and the chisel edge to paint woodgrain lines. Shade the roof with Lamp Black. With Light Buttermilk, apply highlights to the peak and right side of the roof, the right side of the house, the left of the star opening and a few wood grain streaks.

[11] DETAIL THE BIRDHOUSE

Using a no. 10 flat/shader side-loaded with Deep Midnight Blue, glaze tints here and there on the front of the birdhouse. Using an 18/0 liner, paint the nail perch on the birdhouse and a few grain lines on the front and the roof. Then side load a no. 10 flat/shader with Mississippi Mud and shade the edge of the star-shaped opening.

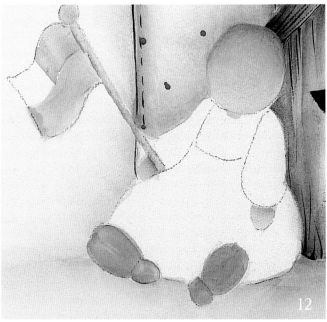

[12] SHADE AND HIGHLIGHT DOLL HEAD AND HANDS

Shade and highlight the head and hands of the doll with a side-loaded no. 10 flat/shader. Use Dusty Rose + Traditional Burnt Sienna for shading and Light Buttermilk for highlighting.

[13] PAINT FACE AND HAIR

Using an 18/0 liner and Lamp Black, paint the doll's eyes and mouth. Using the same brush, wash in the nose and float the lip with Rookwood Red. Using the same color, drybrush scrub (see page 15) the cheeks with a ¼-inch (6mm) DM stippler.

Using an 18/0 liner, paint the hair with Lamp Black, Burnt Umber and Burnt Umber tipped in Fawn, moving in and out of the colors.

[14] PAINT DRESS BODICE

Use a side-loaded no. 10 flat/shader to shade and highlight the doll's dress bodice. Shade with Mississippi Mud and highlight with Warm White. Using an 18/0 liner, paint the heart and stitching around the neck in Deep Midnight Blue.

[15] STRIPE AND SHADE SLEEVES

Using an 18/0 liner, stripe the sleeves with Rookwood Red. Then use a side-loaded no. 10 flat/shader to shade the sleeves in Rookwood Red and highlight in Warm White.

[16] PAINT SKIRT AND SHOES

Stripe the skirt with a no. 2 flat/shader and washy Deep Midnight Blue. Add Rookwood Red stripes between the blue strips, using an 18/0 liner. Using a side-loaded no. 10 flat/shader, shade the waist and right side of the skirt with Deep Midnight Blue and highlight the left side of the skirt with Warm White. Paint the bow at the waist with an 18/0 liner and Deep Midnight Blue.

Using a side-loaded no. 10 flat/shader, shade the shoes in Lamp Black and highlight in Warm White.

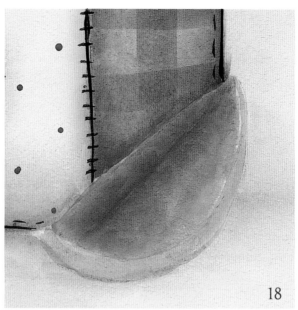

[17] PAINT THE DOLL'S FLAG

Use a no. 10 flat/shader to shade and highlight the doll's flag and the ball on the end of the flag pole. Shade the blue square with Deep Midnight Blue, the red squares with Rookwood Red and the white square with Mississippi Mud. Highlight all the squares with Warm White. Shade the ball on the pole with Burnt Umber. Drybrush stencil the star with a ¼-inch (6mm) DM stippler and Warm White. Add stitchery along the flag squares with an 18/0 liner and Lamp Black. With the same brush and Burnt Umber, darken the flag pole if necessary.

[18] PAINT WATERMELON MEAT

Using a no. 10 flat/shader side-loaded with Rookwood Red, shade along the top edge of the watermelon with a dabby side-by-side float (see page 14). Tip the same brush into Rookwood Red + Light Buttermilk and float above the rind.

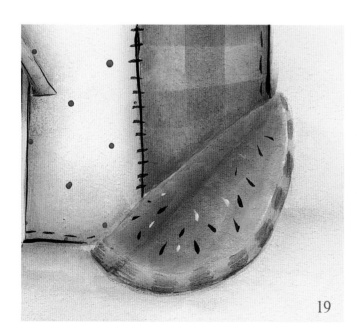

[19] PAINT RIND AND SEEDS

Use a side-loaded no. 10 flat/shader to float Light Avocado + Light Buttermilk along the rind. Shade toward the left with side-loaded Plantation Pine. Use an 18/0 liner and Plantation Pine to line the bottom of the rind and to paint the rind stripes. Each stripe is a series of horizontal lines. Using an 18/0 liner, paint seeds in Lamp Black and in Light Buttermilk.

[20] ADD THE VINE

Use a no. 0 liner and Burnt Umber to paint the vines. Then fully load a no. 8 flat/shader in Light Avocado, side load in Plantation Pine and add stroke leaves (see page 17) .

Let dry and then finish the surface in the appropriate manner (see pages 10-11).

Autumn Wreath

SHORTENED DAYS, CRISP AIR, and leaves of red and gold signal the season's turn to autumn. To enhance the autumn scene, try painting the wheat stalks around the entire wreath. Also try altering the light-colored outside background to a rich gold or green. It's amazing what changing a color can do to a project!

I love to experiment, and I can envision the outer background of each seasonal wreath painted in rich hues to reflect a particular time of year—green for spring, gold for summer, red for autumn and blue for winter. Beautiful!

Materials

LOEW-CORNELL BRUSHES

Flat/wash, series 7550
- ½-inch (13mm)
- ¾-inch (19mm)
- 1-inch (25mm)

Flat/shader, series 7300C
- No. 4
- No. 8
- No. 10

Filbert, series 7500C
- No. 6
- No. 8
- No. 10

Maxine's oval mop, series 270
- ¾-inch (19mm)

Liner, series 7350C
- 18/0

Script liner, series 7050
- No. 1

Round Stroke, series 7040
- No. 2
- No. 4

Debbie Mitchell (DM) stippler, series DM
- ⅛-inch (3mm)
- ¼-inch (6mm)
- ⅜-inch (10mm)

ADDITIONAL MATERIALS

- Basics (See list on page 8.)
- Painting surface of your choice, about 12" x 15" (31cm x 38cm)
- Preparation and finishing materials appropriate for your painting surface (See pages 10-11.)
- Spattering materials: toothbrush and paper to cover painting.

Pattern on page 123.

Pattern on page 123.

PAINT: DECOART AMERICANA ACRYLICS

Antique White

Burnt Orange

Burnt Umber

Buttermilk

Fawn

Golden Straw

Jade Green

Lamp Black

Light Avocado

Light Buttermilk

Light French Blue

Mississippi Mud

Plantation Pine

Raw Sienna

Traditional Burnt Sienna

Uniform Blue

Yellow Ochre

[1] PREPARE, TRANSFER AND BASE

Prepare your painting surface (see pages 10-11). Paint the background with a 1-inch (25mm) flat/wash double-loaded with Antique White and Light Buttermilk and slip-slapped on the surface. Transfer the wreath inset and the major landscape elements. Base the grassy ground with a no. 10 filbert and Jade Green. Pick up some Antique White on the dirty brush and blend on the palette. Then brush the color on the grassy area with crisscross strokes. Base the sky with a no. 10 filbert and slip-slapped Light French Blue. Using a no. 8 filbert, base the sun with Yellow Ochre, the path with Fawn and the pumpkin with Yellow Ochre. Base the pumpkin stem with a no. 2 round stroke and Fawn and the leaves with a no. 6 filbert and Yellow Ochre.

[2] ENHANCE SKY

Using a ¾-inch (19mm) flat/wash, make a brush mix of Light French Blue + Light Buttermilk and float a horizon line just above the hills. Use a ¾-inch (19mm) mop brush to soften the float. With a ¾-inch (19mm) flat/wash, float the clouds in with Light Buttermilk. Shade the upper edge of the sky area with a float of Uniform Blue on a ¾-inch (19mm) flat/wash.

[3] PAINT SUNRAYS

Float all around the sun with a side load of Yellow Ochre on a ¾-inch (19mm) flat/wash to create a glow. Using the same brush, make a brush mix of Raw Sienna + Traditional Burnt Sienna and stutter float (see page 13) around the sun to create sunrays.

[4] SHADE AND HIGHLIGHT SUN

With a ½-inch (13mm) flat/wash, make a brush mix of Raw Sienna and Traditional Burnt Sienna. Float shading along the bottom part of the sun. With the same brush, highlight the top part of the sun with a brush mix of Yellow Ochre + Light Buttermilk.

[5] SHADE AND HIGHLIGHT LOWER GROUND

Shade the lower ground area and along the path's edges with a brush mix of Plantation Pine + Light Avocado on a no. 10 flat/shader. Walk the color into the grassy areas with a dabby float (see page 13) to create texture. Deepen the darker areas of the grass with Plantation Pine on a ½-inch (13mm) flat/wash. With the same brush, highlight the sunny parts of the fields with Yellow Ochre. Start at the top of the field and walk the highlight down with a back-and-forth brush motion.

[6] SHADE, HIGHLIGHT AND TAP IN LEFT CROPS

For the cultivated fields in the background, transfer the pattern of the crop rows so your rows are evenly placed on and over the hills. Also trace the placement of the fir trees along the tops of the hills. With a no. 10 flat/shader and Raw Sienna, float a shade along the bottom of the hills on the left side. Highlight the hilltops with Yellow Ochre. Load a no. 2 round stroke with washy Burnt Umber and tap in the crop rows on the left side. While they're wet, tip the brush into Antique White and highlight the rows. Float a shade of Raw Sienna along both sides of the rows using a no. 8 flat/shader.

[7] SHADE, HIGHLIGHT AND TAP IN CROPS ON RIGHT HILL

With a ½-inch (13mm) flat/wash, float a shade along the bottom of the right hill with Light Avocado. Then float over that with a tint of Raw Sienna. Highlight the top of the hill with Yellow Ochre. Load a no. 2 round stroke in washy Plantation Pine and tip into Jade Green. Tap in the crop rows on the right field. While each row is still wet, tap the row with Raw Sienna. Float a side load of washy Plantation Pine along both sides of the rows to shade, using a no. 8 flat/shader.

[8] SHADE AND HIGHLIGHT PATH, ADD TINTS

With a ½-inch (13mm) flat/wash and Burnt Umber, apply a dabby float to shade along the edges of the path. Highlight down the center of the path with a dabby float of Yellow Ochre. With a side load of Raw Sienna, tint the path with a dabby float to warm up the color with an autumn tone. With a side load of Plantation Pine, tint the areas of the fields where the trees and corn shocks will be to create more texture and interest. Do the same hit-and-miss on the path.

[9] PAINT TRUNKS, BRANCHES AND CORN SHOCKS

Start the deciduous trees by painting the trunks and branches with inky Burnt Umber on a no. 2 round stroke. Pick up Fawn on your brush to highlight and Lamp Black to shade.

With an 18/0 liner, make little thinned puddles of Yellow Ochre, Raw Sienna and Burnt Umber on your palette. Pick up from those puddles to paint in the corn shocks. Switch to a no. 8 flat/shader and float a shade of Burnt Umber above and below the tie around the middle. Float a little bit more shading under the shocks with Plantation Pine.

[10] PAINT FOLIAGE ON LEFT TREE

Begin the fall foliage on the large foreground tree by moistening a ⅜-inch (10mm) DM stippler and double loading with Yellow Ochre + Burnt Orange. Then tap stipple (see page 15) the first layer of leaves. With your dirty brush, tap in a load of Light Buttermilk on the Yellow Ochre side. Tap the load off on your palette, and then stipple in the lightest highlights on the leaves. With a ½-inch (13mm) flat/wash and Traditional Burnt Sienna, float a soft shade along the bottom of the leaves, and deepen here and there among the foliage.

11

12

[11] PAINT FOLIAGE ON RIGHT TREES

For the foliage on the small right tree, double load a moistened ⅜-inch (10mm) DM stippler with Yellow Ochre and Raw Sienna, tap on the palette to blend and tap stipple the first layer of leaves. For the small left tree, follow the same technique, but double load with Yellow Ochre and Traditional Burnt Sienna. Then side load a ½-inch (13mm) flat/wash with Traditional Burnt Sienna and shade at the bottom of both trees and on the right tree where it tucks behind the left tree.

[12] PAINT FIR TREES

Using an 18/0 liner and Burnt Umber, paint the fir trunks. Load the same brush in Plantation Pine and stroke in the branches. Then tip the dirty brush in Jade Green and overstroke the branches again.

13

14

[13] TAP IN SHRUBS

Double load a ⅛-inch (3mm) DM stippler with Plantation Pine and Yellow Ochre and tap in shrubs along the path and around the trees against the far hills and on the grass in the crook of the path.

[14] TAP FLOWERS AND PULL GRASSES

Using an 18/0 liner, tap flowers on the bushes with colors from the palette. With the same brush, pull up grasses of Yellow Ochre around the bushes and the trees, in the tuft of flowers on the grass and in the crook of the path. If necessary, reinforce the grass shading with Plantation Pine side-loaded on a ½-inch (13mm) flat/wash.

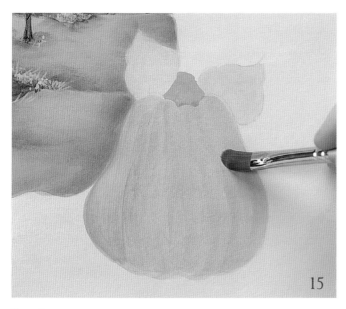

15

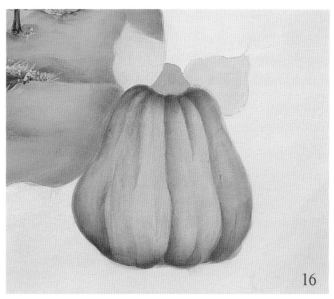

16

[15] WASH OVER PUMPKIN

Using a no. 8 filbert and Traditional Burnt Sienna, add a very light wash over the pumpkin.

[16] SHADE PUMPKIN

With a no. 10 flat/shader side-loaded in a brush mix of Burnt Orange + Traditional Burnt Sienna, shade on both sides of the pumpkin ridges and at the top and bottom of the pumpkin. Deepen the shading with a soft float of side-loaded Burnt Umber.

17

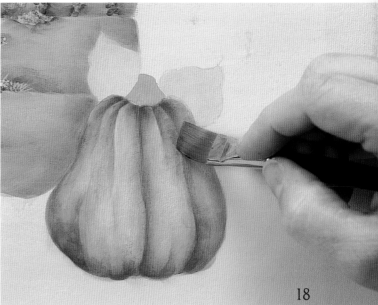

18

[17] HIGHLIGHT PUMPKIN

Load a dry ¼-inch (6mm) DM stippler with Yellow Ochre + a touch of Light Buttermilk, swirl on the palette to blend, and spread pumpkin highlights between the ridges, avoiding the shading. Then float highlighting with the same mix side-loaded on a no. 10 flat/shader.

[18] TINT PUMPKIN

With a no. 10 flat/shader and Plantation Pine, tint with dabby bull's-eye floats (see page 14).

[19] SHADE AND HIGHLIGHT STEM

Shade the pumpkin stem with a no. 8 flat/shader and side-loaded Burnt Umber + Lamp Black. Highlight with a stutter float, using the same brush, side-loaded with Antique White.

[20] SHADE AND TINT LEAVES, ADD VEINS

Using a no. 10 flat/shader side-loaded with Plantation Pine, shade the pumpkin leaves. Note that the shading on the leaf edges tucks into the lobes, leaving space to indicate the veins. With the same brush side-loaded in Burnt Umber, add a tint near the stem. Then add one or two frosty tints on the leaf edges with Yellow Ochre. Switch to an 18/0 liner and pull veins in Plantation Pine.

[21] APPLY A WASH

Side load a 1-inch (25mm) flat/wash with Mississippi Mud and float a wash around the inset and the pumpkin.

[22] PAINT VINE WREATH

Create inklike consistency puddles of Raw Sienna, Burnt Umber and Antique White. Move in and out of these colors with a no. 1 script liner and paint the vine wreath.

[23] SHADE BETWEEN VINES

Shade here and there between the vines with a ½-inch (13mm) flat/wash side-loaded in Burnt Umber. If your shading is applied too intensely, soften it with your finger or with a mop brush.

[24] ADD STROKE LEAVES

Load a ½-inch (13mm) flat/wash with thinned Raw Sienna and paint stroke leaves (see page 17) here and there on the outside of the wreath. Then load the dirty brush into Antique White and paint some leaves inside the wreath.

[25] ADD MORE LEAVES

Add a few leaves in thinned Light Avocado and in Plantation Pine, using a no. 8 flat/shader.

[26] STROKE IN FLOWER PETALS

Undercoat the filler flowers with a no. 4 round stroke and Buttermilk. Let dry. Keep some flowers white; overstroke others with Golden Straw to create a few yellow flowers.

27

[27] PAINT FLOWER CENTERS

Float around the centers of the white flowers with a no. 8 flat/shader side-loaded in Raw Sienna. Do the same for the yellow flowers using Burnt Orange. Paint the flower centers with an 18/0 liner loaded in Burnt Umber and tipped in Raw Sienna.

28

[28] PAINT BERRIES

Paint the Bittersweet berries with a no. 4 round stroke, going in and out of Burnt Orange, Raw Sienna, Traditional Burnt Sienna and Golden Straw. Highlight the tops of the berries with a no. 8 flat/shader and Yellow Ochre.

29

[29] FLOAT GRASS, PULL BLADES

Side load Plantation Pine and a ¾-inch (19mm) flat/shader and float in a grassy area under the pumpkin. Add some Burnt Umber tints. Pull grass blades with an 18/0 liner and Burnt Umber. With the dirty brush, add some Yellow Ochre blades.

30

[30] PAINT WHEAT STALKS

Pull wheat stalks with an 18/0 liner and Burnt Umber. Overstroke with Antique White loaded on the dirty brush. Shade beside the stalks with a ½-inch (13mm) flat/wash and side-loaded Raw Sienna.

[31] ADD WHEAT KERNELS

Stroke in the wheat kernels with a no. 4 flat/shader and Buttermilk. You may need to overstroke to intensify the color. Shade the bottoms of the kernels with Mississippi Mud side-loaded on a no. 8 flat/shader. Paint the filament coming out of the ends of the kernels with Buttermilk on an 18/0 liner.

Cut a sheet of paper roughly to the shape of the wreath and tape it over the wreath. Load an old toothbrush with thinned Burnt Umber and spatter the background (see page 16).

When the painting is dry, finish the surface in the appropriate manner (see pages 10-11).

AUTUMN WREATH (below)

Scaring Up Fun

Wouldn't these whimsical Halloween characters look "boo-tiful" hanging on or near your door to greet guests? Painting a simple "welcome" above or below the characters would add a great touch. Try a black or purple background to make the whole design glow. You can add a few more cobwebs, tucking them in every nook and cranny.

Materials

LOEW-CORNELL BRUSHES

Flat/wash, series 7550
- ½-inch (13mm)
- ¾-inch (19mm)
- 1-inch (25mm)

Flat/shader, series 7300C
- No. 10

Filbert, series 7500C
- No. 6
- No. 8

Liner, series 7350C
- 18/0

Script liner, series 7050
- 18/0

Round stroke, series 7040
- No. 2

Debbie Mitchell (DM) stippler, series DM
- ¼-inch (6mm)

ADDITIONAL MATERIALS
- Basics (See list on page 8.)
- Painting surface of your choice, about 11" x 8½" (28cm x 22cm)
- Preparation and finishing materials appropriate for your painting surface (See pages 10-11.)

Pattern on page 125.

PAINT: DECOART AMERICANA ACRYLICS

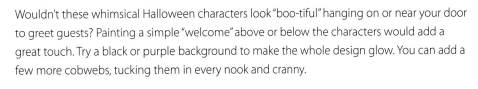

Black Plum	Burnt Orange	Burnt Umber	Buttermilk

Fawn	Jade Green	Lamp Black	Light Avocado

Midnite Green	Neutral Grey	Rookwood Red	Royal Purple

Traditional Burnt Sienna	Warm White	Yellow Ochre

FLOATING TIP

Using a mop brush after you've floated shading, highlighting or glazing helps pick up little imperfections and softens your stroke. Begin in the water area of the float and softly tap the brush up and down, moving in toward the paint.

[1] PAINT BACKGROUND AND BASE

Slip-slap the background with a 1-inch (25mm) flat/wash double-loaded with Light Avocado and Jade Green. Base the pumpkins with a no. 8 filbert and Yellow Ochre. Wash over this with Burnt Orange. (The top pumpkin shows the wash; the bottom pumpkin doesn't.) Base the stem with a no. 2 round stroke and Fawn. With a no. 6 filbert, base the leaves with Jade Green, the ghost with Buttermilk, the bat with Lamp Black, the front of the fence slats with Fawn and the fence slat edges with thinned Burnt Umber. Switch to a no. 2 round stroke and base the main part of the house with Royal Purple, the spider's head with Lamp Black and the spider's body with Burnt Umber. Paint the larger parts of the pumpkins' noses and mouth and the ghost's eyes and mouth with the same brush and Lamp Black. With the same color and an 18/0 liner, paint the smile lines, eye lines, lashes and eyebrows on the pumpkins and the nose, eyelashes and eyebrows on the ghost.

[2] SHADE AND HIGHLIGHT GHOST

Shade the ghost with a ½-inch (13mm) flat/wash side-loaded with Neutral Grey. Deepen the shading with side-loaded Lamp Black. Side load the brush with Warm White for highlighting the ghost's chin, the tops of the sleeves and the body. Apply the body highlight with a bull's-eye float (see page 14).

[3] ADD GHOST DETAILS

Tint the ghost face and body on the left side with Black Plum side-loaded on a ½-inch (13mm) flat/wash. Load a dry ¼-inch (6mm) DM stippler with Rookwood Red and scrub the bristles on the palette and then on a paper towel. Then softly swirl the color on the ghost's cheeks. Use the same color and a no. 10 flat/shader to float a tint under the lip. Paint the vines around the ghost's heart with an 18/0 liner and Burnt Umber.

[4] SHADE AND HIGHLIGHT HOUSE, BEGIN DETAILS

Shade the top and bottom of the house with a no. 10 flat/shader side-loaded in Lamp Black. Highlight the left side with side-loaded Royal Purple + Warm White. Base the house windows with a no. 2 round stroke and Yellow Ochre.

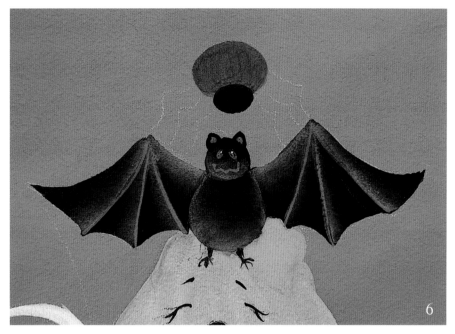

[5] FINISH HOUSE DETAILS

With an 18/0 liner and Lamp Black, line the windows and base the door and roof. Use the same brush to pull a Warm White line on the right of the door and to dot in the doorknob. Highlight the top of the door with Warm White side-loaded on a no. 10 flat/shader.

[6] HIGHLIGHT AND DETAIL THE BAT

Highlight the bat with a no. 10 flat/shader and a brush mix of Neutral Grey + Warm White. With an 18/0 liner, add Neutral Grey wing lines, mouth, eyes, and ear recesses. Tip the brush in Warm White to dot in eye highlights. With the same brush and Lamp Black, add the bat's legs.

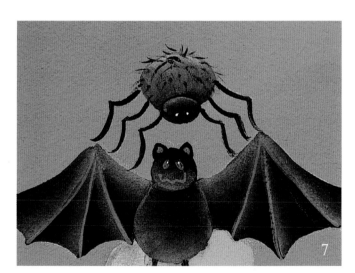

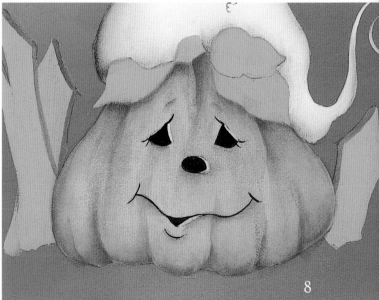

[7] SHADE, HIGHLIGHT AND DETAIL THE SPIDER

Shade behind the head on the spider's body with a no. 10 flat/shader side-loaded with Lamp Black. Side load Yellow Ochre and highlight the spider's backside. Side load with Warm White and highlight the top of the spider's head. With an 18/0 liner and Lamp Black, add hair on the body and paint the legs. Use the brush tip to dot Warm White the eye highlights.

[8] SHADE PUMPKINS

If you haven't yet washed the bottom pumpkin with Burnt Orange, do so now (see step 1). When highlighting and shading the pumpkins, use a ½-inch (13mm) flat/wash for the larger and a no. 10 flat/shader for the smaller. Shade both pumpkins with a side load of Burnt Umber + Traditional Burnt Sienna. This shading goes along the outside edges and vertical indentations. Deepen the shading with Burnt Umber.

9

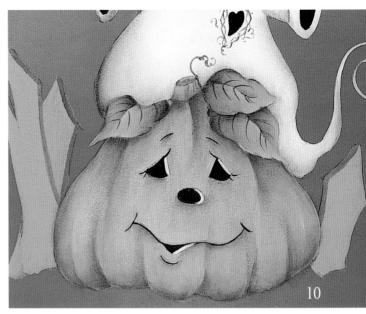

10

[9] HIGHLIGHT PUMPKINS, TOUCH UP FACES

Float Yellow Ochre highlights between the indentations. Then dry-brush scrub (see page 15) the highlights with a ¼-inch (6mm) DM stippler to brighten. If necessary, touch up the "facial" features with an 18/0 liner and Lamp Black.

[10] PAINT PUMPKIN LEAVES, STEM AND CURLICUE

Shade the leaves on both pumpkins with a no. 10 flat/shader side-loaded with Midnite Green. Side load Yellow Ochre for the highlighting and Royal Purple for tints here and there on the leaf edges. Use an 18/0 liner to pull Midnite Green veins.

Shade the stem on the lower pumpkin with Burnt Umber side-loaded on a no. 10 flat/shader. Side load Yellow Ochre for the highlight. Paint the curlicue stem vine with an 18/0 liner and Burnt Umber.

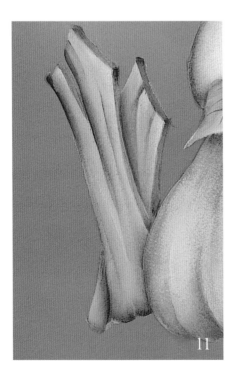

11

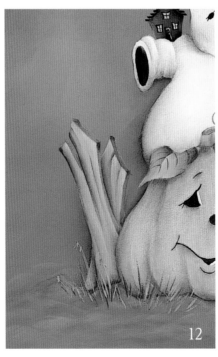

12

[11] SHADE AND HIGHLIGHT FENCE SLATS

Shade the fence slats with a no. 10 flat/shader and side-loaded Burnt Umber. Deepen the shading with Lamp Black on the dirty brush. With Buttermilk side-loaded on the same brush, float in highlights.

[12] PAINT GRASS

Side load a ¾-inch (19mm) flat wash with Midnite Green and float color on the background around the fence slats, pumpkins, ghost and other design items. Don't forget to float under the bottom pumpkin. This shading brings the design forward. With the same brush, float Jade Green over the Midnite Green under the bottom pumpkin. Switch to a ½-inch (13mm) flat/wash and side load Burnt Umber to tint the grassy area. Pull grass blades with an 18/0 script liner loaded with Yellow Ochre + Burnt Umber. Vary the color proportions of the mix.

[13] ADD WEBS

The webs may be done freehand or traced from the pattern. All webs are painted with an 18/0 script liner and Warm White. Don't forget the web string coming out of the spider. Use a ½-inch (13mm) flat/wash to float thinned Warm White along the inside of the outermost web lines. When the painting is dry, finish the surface in the apropriate manner (see pages 10-11).

SCARING UP FUN (below)

Season of Plenty

Materials

LOEW-CORNELL BRUSHES

Flat/wash, series 7550
- ½-inch (13mm)
- ¾-inch (19mm)
- 1-inch (25mm)

Flat/shader, series 7300C
- No. 4
- No. 8
- No. 10

Filbert, series 7500C
- No. 6
- No. 8

Liner, series 7350C
- 18/0

Script liner, series 7050
- 18/0

Round, series 7000
- No. 1

Round stroke, series 7040
- No. 2

Debbie Mitchell (DM) stippler, series DM
- ¼-inch (6mm)

Crescent, series 247
- ⅜-inch (10mm)

ADDITIONAL MATERIALS
- Basics (See list on page 8.)
- Painting surface of your choice, about 11" x 9" (28cm x 23cm)
- Preparation and finishing materials appropriate for your painting surface (See pages 10-11.)

Pattern on page 125.

Celebrate the warmth and blessings of Thanksgiving by painting this cornucopia filled with the bounty of the season. You might paint the entire design on a fabric wall hanging or pick elements from it and paint them on small boxes to tuck here and there in your home. Feel free to change the background colors to suit your decorating tastes. A rich dark green or blue background would look nice, and even changing the color of the birdhouse to a dark red could be interesting.

PAINT: DECOART AMERICANA ACRYLICS

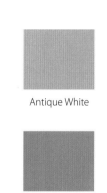

Antique White	Burnt Orange	Burnt Umber	Buttermilk
Fawn	Golden Straw	Hauser Light Green	Lamp Black
Light Avocado	Light Buttermilk	Midnite Green	Milk Chocolate
Payne's Grey	Raw Sienna	Traditional Burnt Sienna	Uniform Blue
Warm White	Yellow Ochre		

DRYBRUSH TIP
Use a light touch as you begin drybrushing and gradually increase the pressure as needed to deposit more color. It's much easier to add color than to remove it.

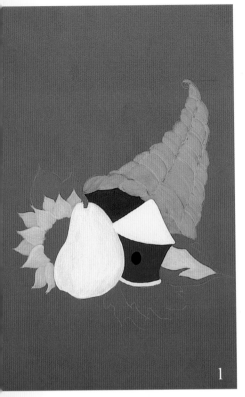

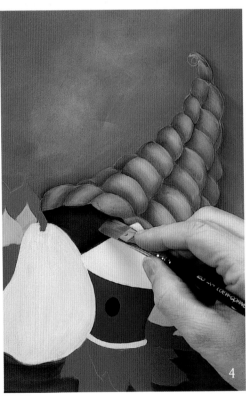

[1] PAINT BACKGROUND AND BASE

Prepare your painting surface (see pages 10-11). Paint background in Raw Sienna with a 1-inch (25mm) flat/wash. Transfer the pattern except for the chickadee. Base the cornucopia with a no. 8 filbert and a thin wash of Fawn. Base the cornucopia opening with a no. 6 filbert and Burnt Umber. Base the gourd with a no. 8 filbert and thinned Buttermilk, leaving the stem the background color. Base the birdhouse with a no. 8 filbert, using Uniform Blue for the sides and Buttermilk for the roof. Switch to a no. 2 round stroke and base the birdhouse bottom in the same color and the birdhouse opening in Lamp Black. Using a no. 6 filbert, base the sunflower petals and corn kernels Golden Straw, and the sunflower leaves and corn husk Light Avocado. Don't base the sunflower center at this point.

[2] GLAZE AND SHADE

Add some glazes around the design. Use a ¾-inch (19mm) flat/wash and premoisten an area with Raw Sienna (background color). Then slip-slap patches of Golden Straw and Raw Sienna on the sides of the cornucopia. Blend out with the dirty brush. Side load the same brush with Traditional Burnt Sienna + Burnt Umber and shade under and to the right of the design elements. Deepen a few areas of the shading with Lamp Black side-loaded on a ½-inch (13mm) flat/wash.

[3] SHADE AND HIGHLIGHT CORNUCOPIA

Using a no. 10 flat/shader side-loaded with Burnt Umber, shade the right, left and bottom of the woven sections of the cornucopia. Scrub highlighting on the upper middle woven sections with side-loaded Buttermilk on a slightly moistened ⅜-inch (10mm) crescent brush.

[4] TINT AND SHADE

With a ¾-inch (19mm) flat/wash and side-loaded Raw Sienna, tint a few areas on the right of the cornucopia's woven sections to warm the color a bit. Shade the opening of the cornucopia with a ½-inch (13mm) flat/wash and side-loaded Lamp Black.

[5] TRANSFER AND BASE CHICKADEE

Transfer the chickadee pattern onto your painting. Do all chickadee basing with a no. 6 filbert. Use thin Buttermilk for the neckband, thin Antique White for the belly and thin Lamp Black for the head and chin area. Fill in the wings and upper and lower body with Lamp Black + Antique White. For the wings, stroke on the chisel edge in the feather direction to create a feathery texture. For the body, pull with the curve of the belly.

[6] SHADE AND HIGHLIGHT CHICKADEE

Do all chickadee shading and highlighting with a side-loaded no. 8 flat/shader. Use Burnt Umber to shade under the black cap and under the black throat areas. Use Lamp Black to shade under the neckband and between the wing feather rows. Highlight the front of the belly, the outer tips of the wings, the top of the head and under the chin with Buttermilk.

[7] ADD FEATHERING LINES

Add feathering lines with an 18/0 liner. Use Lamp Black at the base of the cap into the neckband and at the bottom of the black throat area into the breast. Use Buttermilk from the bottom of the white neckband into the back and along the outside edge of the belly.

[8] PAINT CHICKADEE DETAILS

Paint the chickadee eye, beak, legs and feet with a no. 1 round and Lamp Black. With the dirty brush, highlight the eye with Light Buttermilk. Also with the dirty brush, overstroke the legs and feet with Antique White. Note that the overstroking in the legs is horizontal to show the skin texture. While the beak is still wet, add an Antique White separation line.

[9] SHADE AND HIGHLIGHT SUNFLOWER PETALS

Shade and highlight the sunflower petals with a ½-inch (13mm) flat/wash. Shade at the base of the petals with Raw Sienna + Traditional Burnt Sienna, using a stutter float (see page 13). Highlight with a brush mix of Golden Straw + Light Buttermilk.

[10] PAINT SUNFLOWER CENTER AND LEAVES

Tap stipple (see page 15) the sunflower center with a ¼-inch (6mm) DM stippler and Traditional Burnt Sienna. Let dry. Shade the center with a no. 10 flat/shader side-loaded with brush-mixed Burnt Umber + Lamp Black applied in dabby floats (see page 13) for texture. Highlight with dabby floats, using a brush mix of Raw Sienna + Yellow Ochre.

Use a no. 10 side-loaded flat/shader to shade and highlight the sunflower leaves. Shade with a brush mix of Midnite Green and highlight with Hauser Light Green. Further highlight with a brush mix of Hauser Light Green + Light Buttermilk.

[12] SHADE, HIGHLIGHT AND TINT GOURD

The gourd shading, highlighting and tints are done with a side-loaded ½-inch (13mm) flat/wash. Shade the outside edge of the gourd and beneath the stem with Midnite Green. Highlight with Warm White bull's-eye floats (see page 14) on the left, in the center and on the right edge of the gourd. Using brush-mixed Traditional Burnt Sienna + Burnt Umber add a few bull's-eye-floated tints.

[11] PAINT GOURD STRIPES

Paint stripes on the gourd with a no. 6 filbert and very thin Midnite Green. Swish the brush back and forth to create uneven edges on the stripes.

[13] SHADE AND HIGHLIGHT STEM

Shade the gourd stem with a no. 10 flat/shader and side-loaded Burnt Umber. Highlight with the same brush and side-loaded Yellow Ochre + Light Buttermilk.

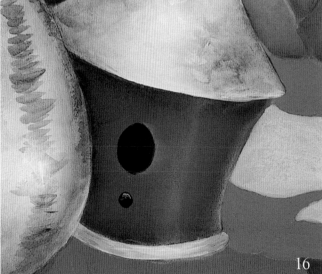

[14] SHADE AND HIGHLIGHT BIRDHOUSE SIDES

Shade the birdhouse sides along the edges with a ½-inch (13mm) flat/wash and side-loaded Payne's Grey. Highlight with side-loaded Uniform Blue tipped with Light Buttermilk. This highlighting appears on the right edge of the birdhouse opening and as a side-by-side float (see page 14) down the right side of the birdhouse.

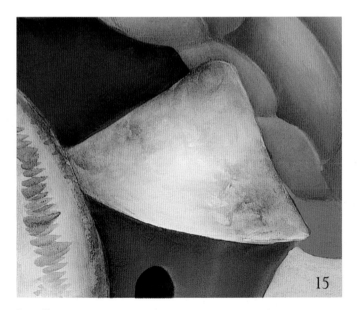

[15] SHADE, HIGHLIGHT AND TINT BIRDHOUSE ROOF

Shade the birdhouse roof with a dabby float of side-loaded Lamp Black loaded on a ½-inch (13mm) flat/wash. Use a no. 10 flat/shader side-loaded in Light Buttermilk to highlight the middle and bottom edges of the roof and to apply a line of backlit highlighting on the roof's right edge. Float bull's-eye tints with a no. 10 flat/shader side-loaded with brush-mixed Burnt Umber + Traditional Burnt Sienna.

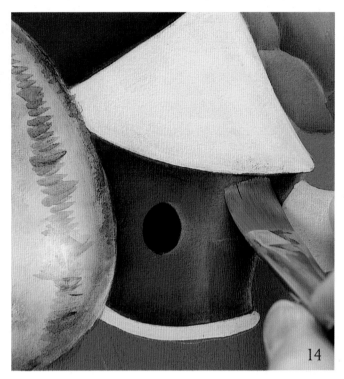

[16] PAINT BIRDHOUSE BOTTOM AND PERCH

Paint the bottom of the birdhouse with thin Yellow Ochre and a no. 6 filbert. While the paint is still wet, streak shading at both ends with Raw Sienna side-loaded on the no. 6 filbert. Side load the same brush with Buttermilk and highlight the middle of the birdhouse bottom. Paint the perch with an 18/0 liner and Lamp Black. Add a Warm White highlight.

[17] SHADE AND HIGHLIGHT CORN

Shade the edges of the yellow corn area and between the kernels with a no. 8 flat/shader side-loaded with Raw Sienna. Deepen the shading with side-loaded Milk Chocolate. Highlight down the middle of the ear, using the same brush and a side-loaded brush mix of Yellow Ochre + Light Buttermilk.

Shade the corn husk with a no. 10 flat/shader side-loaded with Midnite Green. Highlight with the same brush side-loaded with a brush mix of Hauser Light Green + Yellow Ochre.

[18] BASE OAK LEAVES

Base the oak leaves with a no. 6 filbert. For the bottom leaf, use Golden Straw and then paint it again with a dirty brush and Raw Sienna. For the top leaf, move in and out of Burnt Orange and Traditional Burnt Sienna and Yellow Ochre.

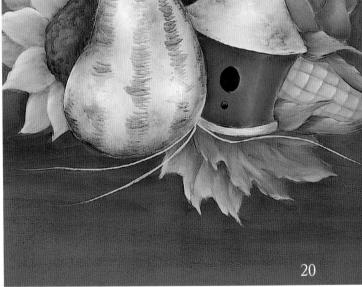

[19] SHADE OAK LEAVES

Use a no. 10 flat to shade and highlight the oak leaves. Shade the bottom leaf with a side-loaded brush mix of Raw Sienna + Traditional Burnt Sienna. Deepen with side-loaded Burnt Umber. Shade the top leaf with side-loaded Traditional Burnt Sienna + Burnt Umber.

[20] HIGHLIGHT LEAF EDGES, PULL WHEAT STEMS

Highlight the outside leaf edges. For the bottom leaf use a side-loaded brush mix of Yellow Ochre + Light Buttermilk. Highlight the top leaf with a brush mix of Burnt Orange + Yellow Ochre.

Pull the main stems of the wheat with an 18/0 script liner and Antique White.

[21] PAINT WHEAT KERNELS AND DETAILS

Stroke in the wheat kernels with a no. 4 flat/shader double-loaded with Antique White and Light Buttermilk. Pull out the wispy filaments with an 18/0 script liner and Antique White. With a ½-inch (13mm) flat/wash, float a Raw Sienna tint at the base of the wheat stems, walking up the stem a bit. When the painting is dry, finish the surface in the appropriate manner (see pages 10-11).

SEASON OF PLENTY (below)

Winter Wreath

I LOVE WINTER!
I love the glistening snow, the smell of gingerbread baking, colorful twinkling lights and the gathering of family and friends. It's the most wonderful time of the year!

This wreath and scene celebrates the lovliness of winter. The mere pressure of your brush can alter the evergreen wreath subtly. If you want to create a bigger wreath, apply more pressure as you stroke on the greenery. For a smaller wreath, apply less pressure. Another way to alter the design is to omit the brown twigs from the wreath. This simple change gives the wreath a whole new look!

Materials

LOEW-CORNELL BRUSHES

Flat/wash, series 7550
- ½-inch (13mm)
- ¾-inch (19mm)
- 1-inch (25mm)

Flat/shader, series 7300C
- No. 4
- No. 8
- No. 10

Filbert, series 7500C
- No. 6
- No. 8

Maxine's oval mop, series 270
- ¾-inch (19mm)

Liner, series 7350C
- 18/0

Script liner, series 7050
- No. 1

Round Stroke, series 7040
- No. 2

Debbie Mitchell (DM) stippler, series DM
- ¼-inch (6mm)

ADDITIONAL MATERIALS

- Basics (See list on page 8.)
- Painting surface of your choice, about 12" x 15" (31cm x 38cm)
- Preparation and finishing materials appropriate for your painting surface (See pages 10-11.)
- DecoArt Snow-Tex
- Spattering materials: toothbrush and paper to cover painting.

Pattern on page 123.

Antique White	Burnt Orange	Burnt Umber	Deep Midnight Blue

Fawn	French Grey Blue	Jade Green	Lamp Black

Light Buttermilk	Midnite Green	Mississippi Mud	Plantation Pine

Rookwood Red	Uniform Blue	Warm White	Yellow Ochre

[1] PREPARE, TRACE AND BASE

Prepare your painting surface (see pages 10-11). Paint the background in a slip-slap manner with a 1-inch (25mm) flat/wash double-loaded with Antique White and Light Buttermilk. Let dry. Transfer the hills, path, inset outline, snowman outline and scarf onto the surface. Using a no. 8 filbert, base the sky Deep Midnight Blue; the hills French Grey Blue, picking up a little Light Buttermilk; and the snowman Light Buttermilk. Base the snowman's scarf with Jade Green loaded on a no. 6 filbert.

[2] FLOAT IN CLOUDS

Side load a ¾-inch (19mm) flat/wash with Deep Midnight Blue + Light Buttermilk and float in cloudy streaks. Soften by swishing over the color with the water side of the brush and with a mop brush.

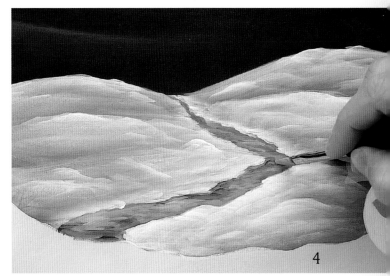

[3] FLOAT SNOW ON HILLS

Side load a ¾-inch (19mm) flat/wash with Light Buttermilk and float frosty snow on the hills. Soften by swishing over the color with the water side of the brush and with a mop. Apply several thin layers. Moving down to a ½-inch (13mm) flat/wash, side load Warm White to further brighten the highlights on the highest areas of the hills and along the path.

[4] BASE PATH

Basecoat the path with a no. 6 filbert and Fawn, occasionally picking up a bit of Burnt Umber to create texture. Move the brush back and forth horizontally.

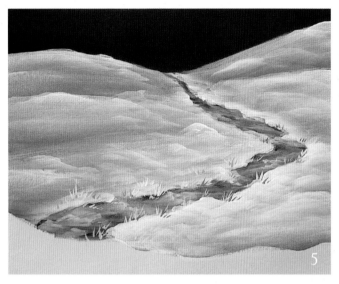

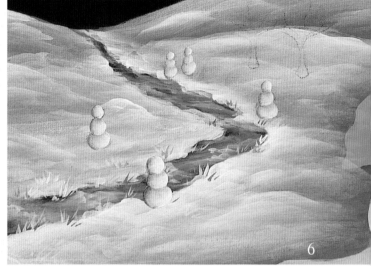

[5] ADD TINTS AND GRASSES

Side load a no. 10 flat/shader with Deep Midnight Blue and add tints here and there along the path. Add Warm White snowy tints in the same manner. Use an 18/0 liner and Warm White + Mississippi Mud to pull up grasses.

[6] TINT, SHADE AND HIGHLIGHT SNOWMEN

Transfer the pattern for the snowmen, firs and the bare trees. Fill in the bodies of the tiny snowmen in the inset with a no. 2 round stroke and Light Buttermilk. Side load Deep Midnight Blue on a no. 8 flat/shader and tint the left side of the snowmen. Then side load the same brush with Mississippi Mud and float shading under the sections of the snowmen to bring out the spherical shapes. Side load the same brush with Warm White and highlight the right side of the snowmen.

[7] DETAIL THE SNOWMEN

Use an 18/0 liner to detail the snowmen. Make the arms Burnt Umber, the eyes and buttons Lamp Black and the carrot noses Burnt Orange. Use palette colors of your choice for the scarves.

[8] PAINT FIR TREES

Use an 18/0 liner for the fir trees on top of the hills. Paint the trunks with Burnt Umber tipped in Fawn. Paint the branches with Plantation Pine tipped in Warm White, pulling the branch strokes down and away from the trunk.

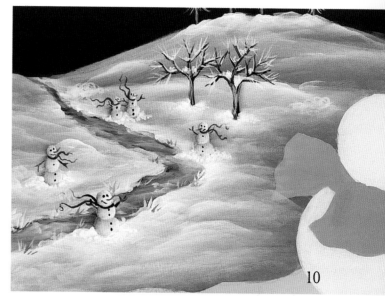

[9] PAINT BARE TREES

Paint the bare trees with an 18/0 liner. For the trunks and branches, go in and out of Lamp Black, Burnt Umber, Mississippi Mud and Warm White. Then overstroke snow on the branches with Warm White. Add a few fine branches with the same color. Use the point of the liner to dot little piles of Warm White snow in the crooks of the branches.

[10] WORK WITH THE SNOW

Using an 18/0 liner and Warm White, tap snow around the bottoms of bare trees and the snowmen. Use the same brush and color to scrub or swirl in snowy bushes here and there on the hills. Side load Warm White on a no. 10 flat/shader and enhance the brightness of the snow. Side load the same brush with Deep Midnight Blue and tuck in shadows along the left side of the snowmen and wherever else you feel a bit of shading is needed to subdue the snow's brightness.

[11] PAINT EVERGREEN BRANCHES

Paint the evergreen branches in the wreath (but not the berry branches) with a no. 1 script liner and inklike consistency Mississippi Mud, Burnt Umber and Light Buttermilk, going in and out of the colors. With a side-loaded ¾-inch (19mm) flat/wash, float Mississippi Mud around the branches.

[12] PULL NEEDLES

Paint the evergreen needles with a no. 10 flat/shader. Double load Plantation Pine and Warm White and, using the chisel edge of the brush, pull needles out and away from all the branches. Then load the same colors and pull needles in toward the branches.

13

14

15

16

[13] PAINT BERRY BRANCHES

Paint the berry branches with a no. 1 script liner. Use Burnt Umber thinned with water to form the branches. Then add Light Buttermilk to the dirty brush and overstroke to highlight. Side load a ¾-inch (19mm) flat/wash with Mississippi Mud and float tints around the branches.

[14] PAINT BERRIES

Fill in the berries with a no. 2 round stroke and a wash of Rookwood Red. Side load a no. 8 flat/shader with Light Buttermilk and float in berry highlights. Use an 18/0 liner to pull fine branches and berry stems. Then use a ½-inch (13mm) flat/wash side-loaded with Rookwood Red to float tints around the berries.

[15] ADD STROKE LEAVES

Add stroke leaves (see page 17) to the wreath with a no. 8 flat/shader and thin Midnite Green. To create enough contrast for the leaves against the sky, use a mix of Midnite Green + Light Buttermilk.

[16] SHADE, TINT AND HIGHLIGHT SNOWMAN

Use a side-loaded ½-inch (13mm) flat/wash for shading, tinting and highlighting the snowman's body. Use Mississippi Mud to shade the top of the head, under the scarf and along the bottom of the snowman. Use Deep Midnight Blue to tint the left side. Use Warm White to highlight on the right of the head and body. With the same color add a bit of backlighting to the left edge of the head and body.

[17] PAINT FACIAL FEATUTES

Transfer the pattern lines for the snowman's facial features, the scarf detail and the birdhouses and poles. Using an 18/0 liner and Lamp Black, paint the snowman's eyebrows, eyes, lashes, mouth and lip line. For the nose, use a no. 2 round stroke and Burnt Orange. While still wet, tap in Light Buttermilk to highlight.

[18] ADD CHEEK COLORING AND LIP TINT

Drybrush scrub (see page 15) the snowman's cheeks, with Rookwood Red on a ¼-inch (6mm) DM stippler. Use a side-load float of Rookwood Red on a no. 8 flat/shader to tint the lower lip.

DRYBRUSH TIP

You don't need to load the brush with much paint for drybrushing—all the scrubbing and swirling is intended to remove most of paint before you apply it to your project.

[19] PAINT HAIR AND ARMS, SHADE

Paint the snowman's hair with an 18/0 liner loaded in Burnt Umber and tipped in Light Buttermilk. Paint the twig arms with a no. 2 round stroke and Burnt Umber. While the paint is wet, overstroke with Light Buttermilk for snow. Using a no. 8 flat/shader side-loaded with Mississippi Mud, shade under the snowman's nose and brows.

20

21

[20] STRIPE AND WEAVE SCARF

Paint the wide stripe on the scarf with a no. 4 flat/shader and Uniform Blue. Add the weave to the stripe with an 18/0 liner and Light Buttermilk. Using the same brush, add thin stripes with Uniform Blue.

[21] SHADE AND ADD FRINGE

Using a side-loaded no. 10 flat/shader, shade the scarf with Midnite Green and highlight with Light Buttermilk. With an 18/0 liner, stroke on Midnite Green fringe. Then shade the fringe area with side-loaded Midnite Green on a no. 10 flat/shader.

22

23

[22] UNDERCOAT AND BASE BIRDHOUSES

Undercoat and base the three birdhouses with a no. 6 filbert and Antique White. Then base the top birdhouse in Uniform Blue, the bottom birdhouse in Yellow Ochre and the middle birdhouse in washy Rookwood Red.

[23] SHADE, HIGHLIGHT AND DETAIL BIRDHOUSES

Shade and highlight the birdhouses with a side-loaded ½-inch (13mm) flat/wash, using Lamp Black for the red and blue birdhouses and Burnt Umber for the tan birdhouse. Highlight the birdhouses with Light Buttermilk. Using an 18/0 liner and Lamp Black, paint the birdhouse posts, roofs, openings, perch and stringy ribbons tied around the posts. Using the same brush, load in Lamp Black, tip in Light Buttermilk and highlight the roofs.

[24] ADD SNOW TEXTURE

Using a side-loaded ¾-inch (19mm) flat/wash, float Warm White under the large snowman and the yellow birdhouse. Then side load a ½-inch (13mm) flat/wash with Snow-Tex and add a bit of the gritty texture under all the snowmen, in the body highlight area of the large snowman, under the tan birdhouse, on the hill highlight areas and on the evergreen wreath needles.

Cut a sheet of paper roughly in the shape of the wreath and tape it over the wreath. Load a toothbrush with thinned Burnt Umber and spatter the background (see page 16). Remove the tissue and spatter Warm White snowflakes inside the wreath. Don't worry if spatters go on the wreath or the background.

When the painting is dry, finish the surface in the appropriate manner (see pages 10-11).

WINTER WREATH (below)

The Snow Family

Meet the Snow family, sitting atop their festive gifts. One of their little ones has lost his head (oh my!), so Mom and Dad are trying to repair him with some fluffy snow. Perhaps you can relate to "losing your head" during the hustle and bustle of the holiday season.

In this design, the airy twig wreath breaks up the background, and snow spattered over the entire scene gives a sparkly effect. Consider painting this design on an ornament box and then picking separate elements to paint on small ornaments that can be stored inside the box.

Materials

LOEW-CORNELL BRUSHES

Flat/wash, series 7550
- ½-inch (13mm)
- ¾-inch (19mm)
- 1-inch (25mm)

Flat/shader, series 7300C
- No. 2
- No. 4
- No. 8
- No. 10

Filbert, series 7500C
- No. 6

Liner, series 7350C
- 18/0

Script liner, series 7050
- 18/0

Round, series 7000
- No. 3

Debbie Mitchell (DM) stippler, series DM
- ⅛-inch (3mm)
- ¼-inch (6mm)

ADDITIONAL MATERIALS
- Basics (See list on page 8.)
- Painting surface of your choice, about 11" x 9" (28cm x 23cm)
- Preparation and finishing materials appropriate for your painting surface (See pages 10-11.)
- DecoArt Snow-Tex
- Toothbrush

Pattern on page 125.

PAINT: DECOART AMERICANA ACRYLICS

Burnt Umber

Buttermilk

Deep Midnight Blue

Fawn

French Mauve

Jade Green

Lamp Black

Light Buttermilk

Light French Blue

Mauve

Mississippi Mud

Plantation Pine

Rookwood Red

Warm White

Yellow Ochre

SNOW TEXTURING TIP

When using DecoArt Snow-Tex medium to give your snow texture, dilute the medium with a bit of water before you begin floating. This breaks down the thickness of the medium and allows easier spreading.

[1] PAINT BACKGROUND AND BASE

Prepare your paint surface (see pages 10-11). Paint the background with Deep Midnight Blue and a 1-inch (25mm) flat/wash. Paint all basecoats with a no. 6 filbert. Base the snowpeople and the ribbon on the left gift in Light Buttermilk. Base the left scarf and center gift in Jade Green. Base the right scarf in French Mauve and the left gift in Mauve + Light Buttermilk (1:1). Base the bow on the center gift in Buttermilk. Base the right gift in Light French Blue.

[2] SHADE, TINT AND HIGHLIGHT SNOWPEOPLE

Shade, tint and highlight all the snowpeople with a ½-inch (13mm) side-loaded flat/wash. Shade the tops and bottoms of the snow-people snowballs with Mississippi Mud; tint on the right with Deep Midnight Blue; highlight on the left with Warm White. Backlight portions of the left edges of the snowpeople with Warm White side-loaded on a no. 10 flat/shader.

[3] PAINT FACES

Transfer the pattern for the snowpeople's faces and buttons (or you may prefer to paint these items freehand). Paint the snowpeople's eyes, lashes, brows and mouth with Lamp Black and an 18/0 liner. Paint the nose with the same brush and Rookwood Red. Drybrush scrub (see page 15) the cheeks with Rookwood Red on a ⅛-inch (3mm) DM stippler.

[4] TINT AND SHADE

Use an 18/0 liner loaded in Burnt Umber and tipped in Fawn to pull in the hair and the twig arms. Dot in the buttons with Lamp Black and a stylus. Shade under the buttons with Mississippi Mud and a no. 10 flat/shader. Add tiny specks of highlighting to the eyes, buttons and the lower snowman's mouth with an 18/0 liner and Warm White. Using the same brush, paint the heart on the lower snowman with Rookwood Red.

[5] PAINT LEFT SCARF

Paint the plaid lines on the left scarf with an 18/0 script liner and Deep Midnight Blue. Shade with a side-loaded ½-inch (13mm) flat/wash and Plantation Pine. Highlight with side-loaded Light Buttermilk. Add fringe with an 18/0 liner and Deep Midnight Blue. Then pick up a touch of Light Buttermilk on the dirty brush and overstroke the part of the scarf fringe against the dark background for contrast. Note the direction of the fringe curve.

[6] PAINT THE RIGHT SCARF

Pull Light Buttermilk and Rookwood Red stripes on the right scarf with an 18/0 liner. Using a ½-inch (13mm) flat/wash, shade the scarf in side-loaded Rookwood Red and highlight in side-loaded Warm White. Pull the fringe with an 18/0 liner and Rookwood Red.

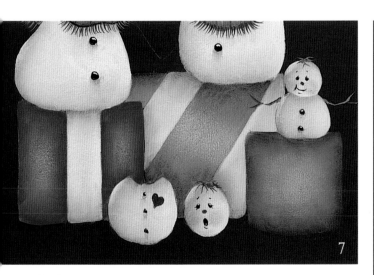

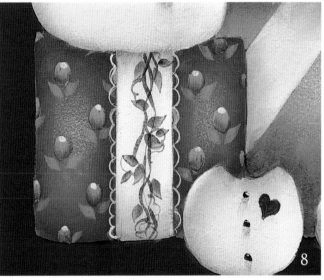

[7] SHADE AND HIGHLIGHT GIFTS

Shade all the gifts and the white ribbons with a side-loaded ½-inch (13mm) flat/wash. Use Rookwood Red for the red gift, Plantation Pine for the green gift, Deep Midnight Blue for the blue gift and Mississippi Mud for the ribbons. Highlight the gifts by drybrushing Light Buttermilk with a ¼-inch (6mm) DM stippler. Highlight the white ribbons with a ½-inch (13mm) flat/wash side-loaded with Warm White. Refer to the photo for the placement of all highlighting.

[8] DECORATE THE RED GIFT

Use a no. 3 round and French Mauve to base the roses on the red gift. Shade the bottoms of the roses with a no. 8 flat/shader side-loaded in Rookwood Red. Tip an 18/0 liner in Light Buttermilk and place a dot at the top of each rose. Paint stroke leaves on the roses (see page 17) with a no. 2 flat/shader and Jade Green.

Paint the vines on the red gift's ribbon with an 18/0 liner and Burnt Umber. Paint stroke leaves with a no. 2 flat/shader and Plantation Pine. Paint the scalloped ribbon trim with an 18/0 liner and Warm White.

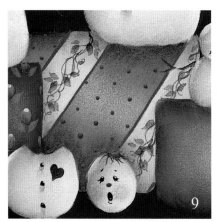

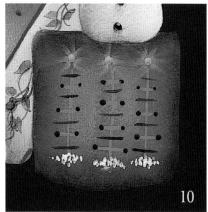

[9] DECORATE GREEN GIFT

Paint the vines on the green gift's ribbon with an 18/0 liner and Plantation Pine. With the same color, paint stroke leaves with a no. 2 flat/shader. Paint lines along the ribbon edges with an 18/0 liner and Mauve. Then add Mauve stylus dots on the green stripes.

[10] DECORATE BLUE GIFT

You may either paint the "tree" design on the blue gift freehand or transfer the pattern. Paint the tree trunks with an 18/0 liner and Fawn. With the same brush, paint the horizontal lines representing tree branches in alternating Jade Green and Plantation Pine. Paint Yellow Ochre stylus dots on the treetops. Stutter float (see page 13) star rays around the dots with a no. 8 flat/shader side-loaded in Yellow Ochre. Use an 18/0 liner and Warm White to dot snow beneath the trees.

[11] PAINT BOWS

Paint the bow on the bottom snowman with an 18/0 liner loaded in Lamp Black and tipped in Warm White. Paint the bow on the right snowman with the same brush loaded in Rookwood Red and tipped in Warm White.

[12] PAINT SNOW, HEART AND OTHER TWIGS

Using the ¾-inch (19mm) flat/wash, float snow on the ground. Then switch to a ½-inch (13mm) flat/wash and float more snow close to the gifts and snowpeople. Also float snow on top of and over the sides of the gifts and in the "hands" of the large snowpeople.

With an 18/0 script liner, stroke thinned Fawn + a touch of Burnt Umber to create a twig-like perimeter around the heart. Mix heavier on the Fawn so the paint will show on the background. Then paint twigs coming from the heart. Also paint the twigs on the ground. For those lying on the snow, mix heavier with Burnt Umber.

With a ¾-inch (19mm) flat/wash float an "aura" outside the perimeter of the heart. With scant Warm White loaded on a dry ¼-inch (6mm) DM Stippler, drybrush scrub (see page 15) a soft glow in the middle of the heart wreath. Paint the leaves on the dark background with a no. 4 flat/shader and Jade Green. For the leaves on the light background, use a mix of Jade Green and Plantation Pine on the dirty brush.

[13] ADD SNOW TEXTURE AND SPATTER FLAKES

To give the snow texture and added highlight, moisten a ½-inch (13mm) flat/wash and side load it with a small amount of Snow-Tex. Apply the Snow-Tex in the brightest part of the snow, which is generally toward the top edges. Also float a few gritty dots in the bodies of the snowpeople. Then toothbrush spatter (see page 16) Warm White snowflakes over the painting.

When the painting is dry, finish the surface in the appropriate manner (see pages 10-11).

THE SNOW FAMILY (below)

Holiday Tree

This snowy tree glowing with colored lights makes a nice variation of the typical green Christmas tree design. Taking cover beneath the boughs is a frosty little gingerbread girl, all decked out in icing.

I can see this design painted on a sled propped next to the fireplace—or maybe on a box for storing Christmas cards. If you want to experiment with colors, a light blue and white mottled background would look lovely. For a simpler design, try painting just the tree or just the gingerbread girl.

Materials

LOEW-CORNELL BRUSHES

Flat/wash, series 7550
- ³⁄₄-inch (19mm)
- 1-inch (25mm)

Flat/shader, series 7300C
- No. 4
- No. 8
- No. 10

Filbert, series 7500C
- No. 6
- No. 8

Script liner, series 7050
- 18/0

Round stroke, series 7040
- No. 2

Debbie Mitchell (DM) stippler, series DM
- ¹⁄₈-inch (3mm)

ADDITIONAL MATERIALS

- Basics (See list on page 8.)
- Painting surface of your choice, about 11" x 8" (28cm x 20cm)
- Preparation and finishing materials appropriate for your painting surface (See pages 10-11.)
- American Traditional Stencils brass template MS-162 (snowflakes)
- DecoArt Snow-Tex
- Toothbrush

Pattern on page 125.

PAINT: DECOART AMERICANA ACRYLICS

 Antique Mauve

 Burnt Umber

 Honey Brown

 Lamp Black

 Light Mocha

 Midnite Green

 Mink Tan

 Sable Brown

 Uniform Blue

 Warm White

PAINT THINNING TIP
Adding water to acrylic paint thins it down and gives it a watercolor effect. This is useful for washes.

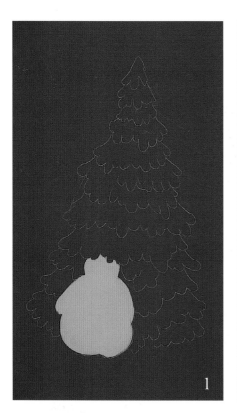

[1] PAINT BACKGROUND AND BASE

Prepare your painting surface appropriately (see pages 10-11). Paint the background with Uniform Blue and a 1-inch (25mm) flat/wash. Basecoat the gingerbread girl with Mink Tan on a no. 6 filbert.

[2] TRANSFER DESIGN AND PAINT FROSTING

Transfer the pattern for the facial features, arms and the heart design on the gingerbread girl. Using a no. 2 round stroke and Light Mocha, paint the gingerbread frosting.

[3] SHADE, HIGHLIGHT AND TINT

Use a no. 10 flat/shader to shade, highlight and tint the gingerbread girl. Shade with Sable Brown + Burnt Umber, highlight with Light Mocha and tint with Antique Mauve.

[4] PAINT FACE AND RIBBON TIE

Use an 18/0 script liner and Lamp Black to paint the gingerbread girl's eyes, mouth and lip line. With the tip of the brush, dot in Warm White eye highlights. With the same brush, paint the ribbon tie in Light Mocha. Drybrush scrub (see page 15) the cheeks with a ⅛-inch (3mm) DM stippler and Antique Mauve.

[5] FLOAT SNOW
Using a ¾-inch (19mm) flat/wash and thinned Warm White, float snow under the tree and gingerbread girl. Follow with floats of Warm White, using the no. 10 flat/shader.

[6] STROKE ON THE BRANCHES
Using a no. 8 filbert loaded in Warm White, stroke on the tree branches, tipping the brush on the edge as you pull the strokes upward. Wash over the branches with the same brush and thinned Warm White

WASH TIP
Err on the side of having a wash be too light rather than too dark. It's much easier to add color than to remove it.

[7] SHADE AND FLOAT

Shade under the branches (and around the gingerbread girl) with Midnite Green and a no. 10 flat/shader. Use the same brush with a side load of Warm White to float along the edges of the tree branches in a scallop effect.

[8] DOT LIGHTS AND FLOAT HALOS

Dot lights on the tree branches with a stylus. Use Antique Mauve, Uniform Blue, Honey Brown and Midnite Green. Then float a halo of color around each dot with a side-loaded no. 8 flat/shader. Make each halo the same color as its dot of light.

[9] ADD VINE AND LEAVES

You may paint the vine freehand, but if you prefer to use the pattern, transfer it at this time. Stroke the vine around the tree with thinned Warm White and an 18/0 script liner. Then add small stroke leaves (see page 17) along the vine with a no. 4 flat/shader loaded with Warm White.

[10] STENCIL SNOWFLAKES

Stencil the snowflakes here and there in the sky area with a ⅛-inch (3mm) DM stippler and Warm White. Tap the brush slightly on a damp paper towel before stenciling.

[11] SPATTER AND ADD TEXTURE

Spatter over the entire scene with thinned Warm White and a toothbrush (see page 16). If you want the snow to have texture, side load a moistened no. 10 flat/shader with Snow-Tex, and apply it here and there on the ground and on some of the tree branches. When the painting is dry, finish the surface in the appropriate manner (see pages 10-11).

HOLIDAY TREE (above)

patterns

Patterns on these two pages may be hand-traced or photocopied for personal use only. Enlarge first at 200 percent and then at 114 percent to bring up to full size.

SPRING WREATH
Pages 22-31

SUMMER WREATH
Pages 56-65

AUTUMN WREATH
Pages 74-85

WINTER WREATH
Pages 100-109

patterns

Patterns on these two pages may be hand-
traced or photocopied for personal use only.
Enlarge at 200 percent to bring up to full size.

LOVE LETTERS
Pages 32-39

LUCKY LEPRECHAUN
Pages 40-45

AMERICANA
Pages 66-73

BUNNY TAKES A BREATHER
Pages 46-55

SCARING UP FUN
Pages 86-91

SEASON OF PLENTY
Pages 92-99

HOLIDAY TREE
Pages 116-121

THE SNOW FAMILY
Pages 110-115

resources

PAINTING SUPPLIES

DecoArt
(For paints and mediums)
P.O. Box 386
Stanford, KY 40484
Phone: 800.367.3047
www.decoart.com

Loew-Cornell
(For brushes)
563 Chesnut Avenue
Teaneck, NJ 07666
Phone: 201.836.7070
www.loew-cornell.com

Masterson Art Products, Inc.
(For wet palette)
P.O. Box 11301
Phoenix, AZ 85017
Phone: 800.965.2675
www.mastersonart.com

SURFACES

Artist's Club
P.O. Box 8930
Vancouver, WA 98668-8930
Phone: 800.845.6507
www.ArtistsClub.com

Catalina Cottage
1968 Essex Court
Redlands, CA 92373
Phone: 866.848.8653
www.catalinacottage.com

Painter's Paradise
C-10 950 Ridge Road
Claymont, DE 19703-2553
Phone: 302.798.3897
www.paintersparadise.com

Stan Brown Arts & Crafts
13435 NE Whitaker Way
Portland, OR 97230
Phone: 800.547.5531
www.stanbrownartsandcrafts.
com

Treasures of the Heart
119 South Old Pacific Highway
Myrtle Creek, OR 97457
Phone: 888.346.0614
www.treasureoftheheartonline.
com

Valhalla Designs
P.O. Box 486
Glendale, OR 97442
Phone: 541.837.3296
www.ValhallaDesigns.com

Viking Woodcrafts, Inc.
1317 8th Street SE
Waseca, MN 56093
Phone: 800.328.0116
www.vikingwoodcrafts.com

MISCELLANEOUS

American Traditional Designs
(For brass stencils)
442 First NH Turnpike
Northwood, NH 03261
Phone: 800.448.6656
www. americantraditional.com

Between the Vines, Inc.
(For author's patterns and
teaching schedule)
P.O. Box 278
Myrtle Creek, OR 97457
Phone: 888.813.VINE
www.betweenthevines.com
info@betweenthevines.com

The Society of Decorative Painters
393 N. McLean Boulevard
Wichita, KS 67203-5968
Phone: 316.269.9300
www.decorativepainters.org

CANADIAN RETAILERS

Crafts Canada
107 May Street South
Thunder Bay, ON P7C 3X8
Tel: 888.482.5978
www.craftscanada.ca

Folk Art Enterprises
73 Marsh Street
Ridgetown, ON, N0P 2C0
Tel: 800.265.9434
www.folkartenterprises.net

MacPherson Arts & Crafts
91 Queen Street East
P.O. Box 1810
St. Mary's, ON, N4X 1C2
Tel: 800.238.6663
www.macphersoncrafts.com

*Maureen McNaughton
Enterprises Inc.*
Rural Route #2
Belwood, ON, N0B 1J0
Tel: 519.843.5648
www.maureenmcnaughton.com

*Mercury Art & Craft
Supershop*
332 Wellington Street
London, ON, N6C 4P6
Tel: 519.434.1636

*Town & Country Folk Art
Supplies*
93 Green Lane
Thornhill, ON, L3T 6K6
Tel: 905.882.0199

U.K. RETAILERS

Art Express
1 Fairleigh Place
London N16 75X
Tel: 0870 241 1849
www.artexpress.co.uk

Atlantis Art Materials
7-9 Plumber's Row
London E1 IEQ
Tel: 020 7377 8855
www.atlantisart.co.uk

Crafts World (head office)
No. 8 North Street, Guildford
Surrey GU1 4AF
Tel: 07000 757070

Green & Stone
259 Kings Road
London SW3 5EL
Tel: 020 7352 0837
www.greenandstone.com

HobbyCrafts Group Limited
7 Enterprise Way
Aviation Park
Bournemouth
International Airport
Christchurch
Dorset BH23 6HG
Tel: 01202596100
www.hobbycraft.co.uk

Homecrafts Direct
P.O. Box 38
Leicester LE1 9BU
Tel: (+44)116 2697733
www.homecrafts.co.uk

index

The best in painting instruction and inspiration is from North Light Books!

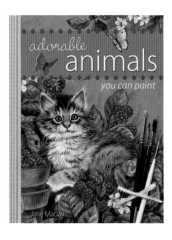

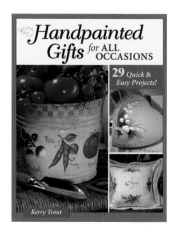

ADORABLE ANIMALS YOU CAN PAINT

You won't be able to resist the cute, cuddly animals in Jane Maday's easy-to-follow painting book. Over 25 step-by-step demonstrations cover a range of skill levels in both acrylic and watercolor. Choose from favorite subjects like kittens, puppies and bunnies as well as some less common but equally lovable subjects like a lamb, sparrow or fawn. You'll also learn how to mix and match Maday's colorful backgrounds with any of her animals—and even how to put your own pet into the picture.

ISBN-13: 978-1-58180-738-7

ISBN-10: 1-58180-738-4, paperback, 128 pages, #33415

A VERY MERRY HANDPAINTED CHRISTMAS

Turn plain, inexpensive glassware into holiday treasures! This book by Carol Mays features over 16 projects to fill your home and your loved ones' hearts with joy. A magical blend of elegance and whimsy, this collection features snowmen, holly, candy canes, fruit and more. It also includes a cookie plate for Santa, porcelain ornaments with country snowscapes, etched wine glasses and a breathtaking set of Christmas Roses tableware.

ISBN-13: 978-1-58180-364-8

ISBN-10: 1-58180-364-8, paperback, 128 pages, #32378

HANDPAINTED GIFTS FOR ALL OCCASIONS

Celebrate the seasons, holidays and family events with 25 quick and easy painting projects by Kerry Trout. You'll find gifts for all of your family and friends, most of which can be made in an afternoon or less. Clear instructions and step-by-step photos make it easy for you to create delightful projects for Mother's Day, Christmas, a new baby and much more!

ISBN-13: 978-1-58180-426-3

ISBN-10: 1-58180-426-1, paperback, 144 pages, #32590

PAINTER'S QUICK REFERENCE: SANTAS & SNOWMEN

Winter may be chilly, but you'll soon warm up to this unique combination of painting instruction and inspiration centered on two favorite winter subjects: Santas and snowmen. Start now on your holiday gifts and decorations with over 20 step-by-step demonstrations and simple projects. You'll find techniques for emphasizing every detail, from Santa's jolly face to a snowman's carrot nose. Easy-to-follow instruction from a variety of artists offers you a wide range of styles and approaches and opens up a winter wonderland of creative possibilities.

ISBN-13: 978-1-58180-614-4

ISBN-10: 1-58180-614-0, paperback, 128 pages, #33184

These and other fine North Light books are available from your local craft retailer and bookstore or from an online supplier.